JOYFUL LIFE BIBLE STUDY

OUR GREAT *Creator*

A study through the book of Genesis

CALVARY PUBLISHING

3232 W. MacArthur Blvd.
Santa Ana, CA 92704

714-979-4422

women.cccm.com

Our Great Creator

A study through the book of Genesis

by Cheryl Brodersen and Jasmine Alnutt

Published by Calvary Publishing
a resource ministry of Calvary Chapel Costa Mesa
3232 W. MacArthur Blvd.
Santa Ana, CA 92704

First printing, 2019

Special thanks to the proofing team, the support board, the leaders and assistants, and to all the wonderful ladies who faithfully attend the Joyful Life Bible study.

Cover layout and design by Andie Overholt.
Cover photo by Nicole Williams.
Internal layout by Angie Emma.

ISBN: 978-1-59751-153-7

Printed in the United States of America.

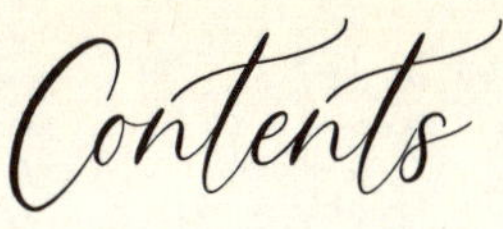

Creation
GENESIS 1–2

FIRST DAY: Introduction

Have you ever asked yourself, *How did I get here?* Usually someone asks this question to bring order and purpose to confusing circumstances. Life itself can seem confusing and meaningless unless we ask the ultimate question, *How did I get here?* The answer to this question is found through studying the book of Genesis. The word *Genesis* means *origin, source,* or *beginning.* This first book of the Bible was given this name because it supplies us with the facts concerning the origin of time, earth, light, plants, animals, mankind, sin, and God's plan for redemption.

Genesis does not endeavor to prove the existence of God, because His existence, power, and genius are evident in His creation. Instead, Genesis presents mankind with the necessary facts to understand:

- How God's good creation was spoiled by the introduction and seduction of sin
- The reason creation and mankind needed redemption through a perfect Savior

As you read Genesis chapters 1 and 2, pay special attention to the purpose, plan, and purity of God's good creation.

Ask God to open your understanding to the purpose of His creation and His plan for your life.

SECOND DAY: Read Genesis 1:1–25

1. Print the first four words of Genesis 1:1.

    a. Link this with John 1:1 and share your thoughts.

2. Genesis 1 tells us the origin of the world. According to Genesis 1:1, what happened *in the beginning*?

    a. Link this with John 1:2. What do you note about creation?

    b. The Hebrew word for *created* is *bara,* which means *to create out of nothing.* The use of this word is exclusively applied to God's work. How does this speak to you?

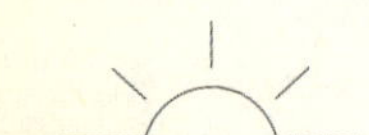

FOOD FOR THOUGHT

Note that in Genesis 1:1–3 the triune nature of God is displayed. God created, the Spirit prepared the world for God's Word, and God's Word (Jesus) brought God's will to pass.

3. Use Genesis 1:2a to describe the condition of the earth.

    a. In Genesis 1:2b the term *hover* in Hebrew speaks of *cherishing or brooding over one's young.* What does this convey to you about the Holy Spirit's activity?

4. In Genesis 1:3–25 God continued His work of creation. Complete the chart below to cite and remark on what God created each *day*:

DAYS	WHAT GOD MADE	RELATED VERSES	OBSERVATIONS
First day (vv. 3–5)		2 Corinthians 4:6	
Second day (vv. 6–8)		Psalm 19:1	
Third day (vv. 9–13)		Psalm 95:5	
Fourth day (vv. 14–19)		Psalm 8:3	
Fifth day (vv. 20–23)		Psalm 104:24–26	
Sixth day (vv. 24–25, 27)		Job 12:7–10; 33:4	

FOOD FOR THOUGHT

Notice that all plant and animal life was created *according to its kind.* Pastor David Guzik says, *It means God allows variation within a kind, but something of one kind will never develop into something of another kind.*[1]

a. Observe that God spoke everything into existence. Link this with John 1:3. What do you see?

5. Six times in this passage we read that God's creation was *good.* How does this minister to you? See also James 1:17.

THIRD DAY: Read Genesis 1:26–31

1. The climax of God's creative work was the creation of mankind on the *sixth day.* According to Genesis 1:26a, what was unique about God's creation of *man*?

    a. Record a few characteristics that are distinct to mankind.

        (1) How does this affect your estimation of other people?

b. Note that God says, *Let **Us** make man in **Our** image.* What does this convey to you about the triune nature of God? See also John 17:5.

2. Use Genesis 1:26b to list the things that man was to have *dominion* over.

   a. Link this with Psalm 8:4–8. What does this communicate to you about man's original role in God's creation?

3. Consider the following aspects of the creation of man from Genesis 1:27 and share why you think each of these is significant:

   a. *In the image of God He created him*

   b. *Male and female He created them*

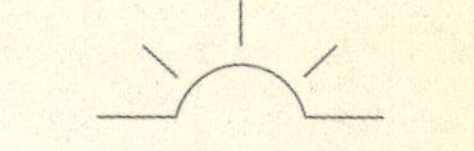

FOOD FOR THOUGHT

In Genesis 1 God is called *Elohim* thirty-two times. This Hebrew word is the plural form of God and denotes His power, majesty, and triunity.

4. After God created mankind, He blessed and instructed them. Use God's words in Genesis 1:28–30 to note and comment on:

    a. Man's role (verse 28)

    b. God's provision (verses 29–30)

5. According to Genesis 1:31, at the end of the *sixth day,* God saw all *He had made, and indeed it was very good.* Take a moment to write a sentence of appreciation for the goodness of God's creation.

FOURTH DAY: Read Genesis 2:1–14

1. In Hebrew literature it is common to provide an overview of an event, followed by a more detailed account. Genesis 1 surveyed all creation, while Genesis 2 focused particularly on the creation of man. After the sixth day of creation, *the heavens and the earth, and all the host of them, were finished.* So on the *seventh day* God *rested* (Genesis 2:1–2). From Genesis 2:3 remark on the uniqueness of the *seventh day.*

a. Link this with the following Scriptures and comment on the:

(1) Physical purpose—Exodus 20:8–11

(2) Spiritual significance—Hebrews 4:9–11

2. Genesis 2:4–6 describes the atmosphere of the earth before the creation of living things. Read these verses and record what stands out to you.

3. Use Genesis 2:7 to recount how *man became a living being.*

a. The word *formed* in Hebrew denotes the work of a potter creating something from clay. What do you find remarkable about this? See also Psalm 139:13–15 and Isaiah 64:8.

4. Genesis 2:8–14 describes the *garden* of Eden, where God put *man*. Read these verses and note what you find interesting about:

   a. Who planted it (verse 8)

   b. The trees of Eden (verse 9)

   c. The river of Eden (verses 10–14)

      (1) Use the meaning of the names of the *four riverheads* to enhance your answer: *Pishon (full flowing), Gihon (bursting forth), Hiddekel (swift), Euphrates (fruitful).*

FOOD FOR THOUGHT

The *Tree of Life* is mentioned prominently in the book of Revelation. Read Revelation 2:7 and 22:2 to discover more.

5. What do you think of God's creation thus far?

FIFTH DAY: Read Genesis 2:15–25

1. According to Genesis 2:15, for what purpose did God place *man* in His *garden*?

2. Use Genesis 2:16–20 to note and comment on what took place in God's *garden*:

   a. God's command to Adam (verses 16–17)

   b. Adam's deficit (verses 18, 20b)

      (1) Notice that this was the first time God said something was *not good*—Adam's loneliness. What does this suggest to you?

   c. Adam's responsibilities (verses 19–20a)

      (1) Bible commentators point out that God was allowing Adam to feel his deficit before creating woman. Why do you think this was necessary?

3. The creation of Eve is given more attention than that of any other creation. Use Genesis 2:21–22 to highlight some of the details of her creation.

    a. How does this enhance your understanding of God's estimation of *woman*? See also 1 Corinthians 11:11–12.

4. Some commentators believe that Genesis 2:23 was the first recorded song. What do you think Adam was communicating through this song?

    a. According to Genesis 2:24, what principle did God establish?

        (1) Link this with Matthew 19:4–6 and Ephesians 5:28–31 and share your thoughts.

5. Genesis 2:25 notes that the man and woman were *naked* and *not ashamed.* Pastor David Guzik explains, *To be naked and unashamed means you have no sin, nothing to be rightly ashamed of, nothing to hide.*[2] What does this reveal about man's original condition?

6. How has your study today spoken to you about:

   a. God's concern for humanity

   b. The glory of woman

   c. Marriage

SIXTH DAY: Review

1. Genesis has rightly been called the *book of beginnings*. From your study this week, share a takeaway concerning the beginning of:

   a. The heavens and earth

   b. Time (day and night)

   c. Plants and animals

d. Mankind

e. Work

f. Rest

g. Marriage

2. Use the following Scriptures to express your appreciation for *Our Great Creator*:

   a. Psalm 33:6–9

   b. Isaiah 45:18

   c. Romans 1:20

   d. Colossians 1:16–17

   e. Hebrews 11:3

3. What is your greatest takeaway from your study this week?

NOTES

NOTES

The Fall
GENESIS 3–5

FIRST DAY: Introduction

Temptation is something every person is familiar with. It is the enticement to do something that violates what we know to be right, good, or in the best interest of ourselves and others. Sometimes we resist, yet sometimes we succumb; the consequences, more often than not, prove disastrous. Understanding the source of temptation, its false promises, and its appeal to our nature is part and parcel of learning to resist it.

Genesis 3 records what is commonly called *The Fall.* It is the tragic story of how God's *good* creation fell from its original perfection and goodness through man's sin and disobedience. Genesis 3 answers the questions of why things are wrong in the world, and why things go wrong in life. When man disobeyed God, tragic consequences ensued and worked death, corruption, sorrow, pain, and decay into God's creation. It is because of this fall, the curse of sin, and man's inability to resist sin, that a Savior was needed. Although God covered Adam and Eve's nakedness with the skin of an innocent animal, the sin of all mankind would necessitate a greater and eternal covering through the blood of Jesus Christ. The first glimpse of God's redemptive work through Jesus was given in Genesis 3:15 when God promised that the *seed* of the woman would crush the serpent's head—this crushing took place on the cross.

The account of the fall is not meant to cause us to blame Adam and Eve but to recognize our own susceptibility to sin and need of a Savior. Jesus has crushed the serpent's head, and now He is working to bring about regeneration and perfection in our lives. Because of Jesus, we can live in the hope that creation will one day be restored to the good and perfect intentions of God.

Ask God to help you see your own susceptibility to temptation and need for Jesus.

SECOND DAY: Read Genesis 3:1–6

1. Genesis 3 records the fall of man and the entrance of sin into the world. Genesis 3:1a tells us that the agent of man's temptation to sin was *the serpent*, who *was more cunning than any beast*. Use the following verses to discover and remark on the true identity and character of this *serpent*:

   a. John 8:44

   b. 1 Peter 5:8

   c. 1 John 3:8

   d. Revelation 12:9–10

2. The *serpent* initiated a conversation with the *woman*. Use Genesis 3:1b–5 to note and comment on how the *serpent* sought to undermine:

   a. God's Word (verse 2)

      (1) Compare Eve's response to the *serpent* (Genesis 3:3) with God's original prohibition (Genesis 2:16–17). What differences do you detect?

b. God's power (verse 4)

c. God's character (verse 5)

3. From Genesis 3:6a, note and comment on the three reasons that convinced Eve to eat the fruit.

   a.

   b.

   c.

      (1) Share a way you would have liked to caution Eve.

4. According to Genesis 3:6b, what did Eve do after she *ate* the fruit?

   a. How did Adam respond?

      (1) What does this convey to you about disobedience and sin?

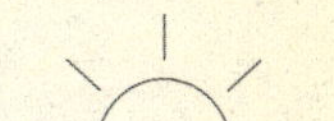

FOOD FOR THOUGHT

From the beginning, Satan has tried to undermine God's people by undermining God's Word.[3]
—Pastor David Guzik

5. Eve did not realize the dangerous character or wiles of her tempter when she conversed with him. Suggest some ways you can recognize Satan's temptations and resist them (See James 4:7).

THIRD DAY: Read Genesis 3:7–13

1. List the consequences that resulted from Adam and Eve's disobedience:

   a. Genesis 3:7

      (1) How does this expose the fallacy of the serpent's promise in Genesis 3:4–5?

   b. Genesis 3:8

   c. Genesis 3:9–10

      (1) What do you find most tragic about these consequences?

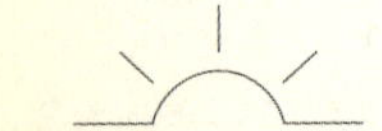

FOOD FOR THOUGHT

Man died spiritually the moment he ate. That is the reason he ran away from God. That is the reason he sewed fig leaves for a covering.[4]
—Pastor J. Vernon McGee

2. Use Genesis 3:11 to write the two probing questions God asked Adam:

   a.

   b.

      (1) Why do you think Adam's awareness of his nakedness was proof of his disobedience?

         (a) Share a way sin makes you vulnerable.

3. How has your study today increased your appreciation for our sinless Savior?

FOOD FOR THOUGHT

Recall that *the LORD God called to Adam* and asked where he was (Genesis 3:9). Dr. W.H. Griffith Thomas says of this, *It is the call of Divine justice, which cannot overlook sin. It is the call of Divine sorrow, which grieves over the sinner. It is the call of Divine love, which offers redemption for sin.*[5]

FOOD FOR THOUGHT

It is interesting that it was by a tree that man lost his fellowship with God, and the cross of Jesus Christ, the tree upon which He was crucified, is the door that can lead a man back to God.[6]
—Pastor Chuck Smith

FOURTH DAY: Read Genesis 3:14–24

1. Sadly, mankind's sin brought about tragic consequences. Use Genesis 3:14–19 to cite and remark on the consequences of sin:

   a. On the *serpent* (verses 14–15)

(1) Pastor Warren Wiersbe points out that verse 15 is *called the protoevangelium ("the first Gospel"), because* [it is] *the first announcement of the coming Redeemer found in the Bible. To the Old Testament covenant people, this verse was a beacon of hope; to Satan, it was God's declaration of war climaxing in his condemnation; and to Eve, it was the assurance that she was forgiven and that God would use a woman to bring the Redeemer into the world.*[7] Link this with the following Scriptures and share your thoughts:

(a) Romans 16:20

(b) Colossians 2:14–15

(c) Hebrews 2:14–15

(2) The word *enmity* in Hebrew means *hatred and hostility.* What does this suggest to you about spiritual warfare?

b. Upon the *woman* (verse 16)

c. For Adam (verses 17–19)

(1) Share a few ways the consequences of man's sin explain the fallen condition of our world today.

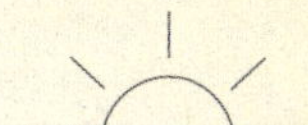

FOOD FOR THOUGHT

Now that death entered the world through sin, the seed of the woman that was unfertilized would die monthly. The fertilized seed of the woman would bring forth life, with pain and discomfort, into a world cursed by death.

2. From Genesis 3:20, remark on why Adam named his wife *Eve*.

a. Genesis 3:21 informs us that in order for God to clothe Adam and Eve sufficiently an animal had to be sacrificed. How do you see this as a foreshadowing of what God would accomplish through Jesus? See also Hebrews 9:22 and 1 John 1:7.

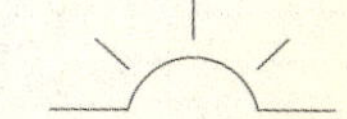

FOOD FOR THOUGHT

Note that God, in His mercy, did not curse Adam and Eve. Instead, they suffered the consequences of their sin. However, the earth and Satan were cursed for the sake of man.

3. According to Genesis 3:22–24, what did God do to prevent Adam and Eve from eating of the *tree of life* and living *forever* in the condition of sin and death?

   a. How do you see this as a mercy?

4. As we see in Genesis 3:15, from the beginning God had a plan for mankind's redemption from sin. Read the following Scriptures to remark on this plan:

   a. Romans 5:14–19

   b. 1 Peter 1:19–20

FIFTH DAY: Read Genesis 4

1. Immediately after they left the Garden of Eden, the consequences of sin began to manifest. Adam and Eve gave birth to their first son, Cain. At his birth Eve said, *I have acquired a man from the Lord* (Genesis 4:1). In Hebrew, this implies that Eve hoped Cain was the promised *seed* of Genesis 3:15 that would break the curse of sin. What do you find interesting about this?

2. After Cain, Eve gave birth to *his brother Abel* (Genesis 4:2a). Use Genesis 4:2b–5a to compare and contrast the two boys in the chart below:

	CAIN	ABEL
Occupation (verse 2b)		
Offering (verses 3–4a)		
God's Perspective (verses 4b–5a)		

a. Read Hebrews 11:4 to understand and comment on the true distinction between Cain and Abel and their offerings.

3. Cain was *very angry* that God did not *respect* his offering (Genesis 4:5b). Genesis 4:6–7 (NLT) says, *"Why are you so angry?" the LORD asked Cain. "Why do you look so dejected? You will be accepted if you do what is right. But if you refuse to do what is right, then watch out! Sin is crouching at the door, eager to control you. But you must subdue it and be its master."* What does this reveal to you about:

   a. Cain

   b. God

   c. Sin

4. Tragically, Cain did not heed God's warning and *killed* his brother Abel (Genesis 4:8). Use Genesis 4:9–15 to remark on the following from Cain's encounter with God:

   a. God's probing questions (verses 9a, 10)

   b. Cain's evasion (verse 9b)

   c. Cain's consequences (verses 11–12)

d. Cain's self-concern (verses 13–14)

e. God's mercy (verse 15)

5. At this point Cain *went out from the presence of the LORD* and into the land of Nod (Genesis 4:16). Genesis 4:17–24 records some of Cain's descendants. Use this record to find a few of the effects of leaving the *presence of the LORD.*

6. According to Genesis 4:25–26a, what took place with Adam and Eve after the death of Abel?

   a. What hope entered the world after the birth of Seth's son Enosh? Genesis 4:26b

      (1) Link this with Proverbs 18:10 and share why this is a good reason for hope.

SIXTH DAY: Read Genesis 5, Review

1. From Genesis 5:1–2, what declaration is restated concerning God's original creation of Adam and Eve?

    a. How does God's original intent contrast with the present fallen state of mankind?

2. Scan the *genealogy of Adam* and his descendants in Genesis 5:3–32, and record any observations.

3. In Genesis 5:21–24 Enoch is given particular attention. Link this with Hebrews 11:5 and Jude 14–15 to further comment on Enoch's significance.

    a. How do you see God's mercy at work in spite of the consequences of sin?

4. While Genesis 3–5 documents the beginning of sin and its effect upon the world, it also offers us the beginning of God's mercy and hope for mankind. From your study this week, share a way you see God's mercy displayed in the lives of:

   a. Adam

   b. Eve

   c. Cain

   d. Seth

   e. Enoch

5. What did this week's study reveal to you about Our Great Creator?

NOTES

The Flood
GENESIS 6–8

FIRST DAY: Introduction

After getting grimy and dirty, there is nothing as refreshing as a good shower! Water is the ultimate solvent for cleansing mud, stains, and debris. It breaks down the stubborn grip of odors and filth and rinses them away.

Ten thousand years ago the earth needed a good shower. Mankind had corrupted the earth to the point that life would be impossible to sustain. Unless the earth received a good cleansing, all nature and mankind would die beneath their spiritual and physical wreckage. As God looked down upon the earth, He searched for anyone He could salvage. Of all mankind, only Noah and his family responded to God's Word. This is how Noah found grace in the eyes of the Lord (Genesis 6:8).

Noah, who had never known rain, obeyed God's specific instructions and built a huge barge called an ark. It took one hundred years to build, and during that time Noah preached to those who scoffed and ridiculed at the notion of divine judgment (2 Peter 2:5). When the ark was finished, God divinely guided animals of every species into the ark. Then God shut the door.

For forty straight days, rain fell from heaven, lifting the heavy barge, covering the mountains, and bringing a thorough cleansing to the whole earth. Jesus referenced Noah when He spoke about the conditions of the earth before His return: *And as it was in the days of Noah, so it will be also in the days of the Son of Man: They ate, they drank, they married wives, they were given in marriage, until the day that Noah entered the ark, and the flood came and destroyed them all* (Luke 17:26–27).

Certainly we are seeing many resemblances to Noah's time proliferating around us. There are those who scoff at the idea of impending judgment. However, those who listen and believe God's Word prepare themselves by receiving and appropriating the salvation offered through Jesus Christ. Even as Noah was saved from the judgment that fell upon the earth, so we are saved by grace from the impending, righteous judgment of God against sin.

Ask God to help you to receive, believe, and obey His Word.

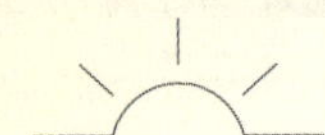

FOOD FOR THOUGHT

Sons of God—This term has never been fully understood. Some say the *sons of God* refers to fallen angels. Others regard these as superior human beings or aristocrats. The third opinion holds that these men were of Seth's lineage (implying that even the godly lineage had become corrupted by men—taking whatever they desired without regard to God or others).

SECOND DAY: Read Genesis 6:1–8

1. It had been about 1,600 years since man was expelled from the Garden. Then as *men began to multiply on the face of the earth,* sin and corruption began to multiply as well. From Genesis 6:1–4 note and comment on this ungodly progression:

   a. Unrighteous unions (verse 2)

   b. Unusual offspring (verse 4)

   c. Unfortunate consequences (verse 3)

2. Genesis 6:5–7 reveals that the spiritual condition of mankind had deteriorated significantly by this time. Use these verses to note and comment on:

   a. Man's condition (verse 5)

   b. God's response (verse 6)

   c. God's remedy (verse 7)

(1) What do you find most striking about this scene?

(2) The judgment God decreed at this time foreshadows a greater future judgment. Read Matthew 24:36–39 and share your thoughts.

3. What was the only hope in the midst of these dismal conditions? Genesis 6:8

   a. Connect this with Romans 5:20b. What parallels do you see between Noah's time and the present conditions in our world?

   b. Why is God's *grace* essential for our time?

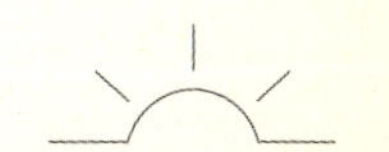

FOOD FOR THOUGHT

Grace—The Hebrew word *chen* means favor or acceptance; good will.

THIRD DAY: Read Genesis 6:9–22

1. Use Genesis 6:9–10 to describe Noah.

FOOD FOR THOUGHT

Genesis 6:9 is the first time the word *righteous* is used in the Bible.

2. Use Genesis 6:11–12 to contrast Noah with the condition of the *earth*.

   a. How do these conditions highlight the uniqueness of Noah?

   b. According to 2 Peter 2:5, Noah was also a *preacher of righteousness* in his generation. Considering the social climate, why is this remarkable?

   c. Link this with the following Scriptures and share a few ways we can follow Noah's example:

      (1) Ephesians 5:6–11

      (2) Philippians 2:15

      (3) 1 Peter 2:9–12

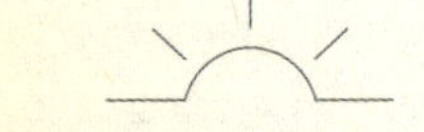

FOOD FOR THOUGHT

Noah wasn't a minor character in the story of redemption; he's mentioned fifty times in eleven different books of the Bible.[8]
—Pastor Warren Wiersbe

3. In Genesis 6:13 God declared to Noah that He would *destroy* all life on earth because of man's profound depravity. However, God had a plan by which He would preserve Noah and his family. Use Genesis 6:13–21 to fill in the chart:

God's Plan	Verses 13, 17
God's Instruction	Verses 14–16
God's Covenant	Verse 18
God's Passengers	Verses 19–20
Noah's Provision	Verse 21
Noah's Response	Verse 22

a. Observe Noah's response to God's Word in Genesis 6:22. Link this with Hebrews 11:7 to remark on the significance of his response.

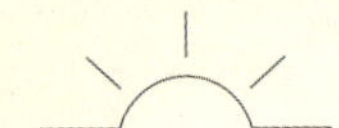

FOOD FOR THOUGHT

The *ark* was about 450 feet long by 75 feet wide by 45 feet high, or close to 1.5 million cubic feet. This could hold about 1,300 standard shipping containers, providing space for about 125,000 animals. Shaped like a barge, the *ark* was exceedingly stable—designed for capacity and floating, not speed and navigation.

b. Bible commentator Matthew Poole pointed out, *The work of building the ark was laborious, costly, tedious, dangerous, and seemingly foolish and ridiculous, especially when things continued in the same posture and safety for … years.*[9] How does this amplify:

(1) Noah's obedience

(2) Noah's faith

4. Although God would judge the wickedness of mankind, He gave opportunity for repentance. Use 1 Peter 3:20 and 2 Peter 3:9 to comment on the *longsuffering* nature of God.

FOURTH DAY: Read Genesis 7

1. From Genesis 7:1 comment on God's invitation to Noah.

2. The Lord told Noah to take *seven each of every clean animal and two each of unclean* animals (Genesis 7:2–3). Seven days later, what would God do? Genesis 7:4

3. Genesis 7:5–24 records the preparation of the *ark* and the coming of the *flood*. Read this account, noting any observations or insights concerning:

   a. Noah

   b. The flood

   c. The results of the flood

   d. God

4. Although God's judgment was thorough and cataclysmic, Noah and his family were preserved. Link this with 2 Peter 2:5, 9. How does this minister to you?

5. Share a time or way you have experienced God's:

   a. Deliverance

   b. Preservation

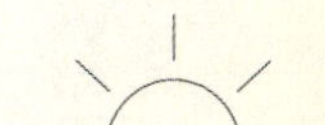

FOOD FOR THOUGHT

Noah was doing just as God had commanded. There seemed to be no problem gathering the animals—God took care of the details of that job while Noah was doing his part, building the ark. Often we do just the opposite of Noah. We worry about details in our lives over which we have no control, while neglecting specific areas that are under our control [like attitudes, relationships, responsibilities]. Try to be more like Noah, concentrating on those things God has given you to do, and leaving the rest to Him.[10]

—Genesis 7:16
Life Application Bible

FIFTH DAY: Read Genesis 8

1. Use Genesis 8:1 to describe God's disposition and activity.

   a. Link this with the following Scriptures and share your heart:

      (1) Psalm 145:9

      (2) Isaiah 49:15–16

2. According to Genesis 8:1b, *God made a wind to pass over the earth.* What happened as a result? Genesis 8:2–5

3. Read Genesis 8:6–14 to summarize how Noah monitored the receding of the floodwaters.

4. In Genesis 8:15–19 God told Noah that it was time for him and *all flesh* that was with him to come out of the ark, *so that they may abound on the earth.* Why do you think it was significant that Noah waited until God commanded him to leave the ark?

5. What was the first thing Noah did upon leaving the ark? Genesis 8:20

   a. What does this suggest to you about Noah?

6. When the LORD *smelled* the offering on the altar, what did He say *in His heart* that He then communicated to Noah? Genesis 8:21–22

   a. Link this with Isaiah 54:9–10. How does this speak to you about:

      (1) God's promises

      (2) God's mercy

      (3) God's preservation

      (4) God's peace

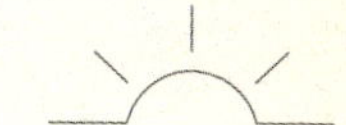

FOOD FOR THOUGHT

Before the flood, the earth was a uniform temperature. After the flood, there would be seasons and yearly changes in the temperature. Mankind would have to adjust to a whole new way of life.

SIXTH DAY: Review

1. From your study this week in Genesis 6–8, share your greatest takeaway concerning:

    a. Sin

    b. Judgment

    c. Righteousness

    d. Grace

    e. Faith

    f. Obedience

    g. The Flood

2. Share any insights you garnered from your lesson this week concerning Our Great Creator.

NOTES

NOTES

God and the Nations
GENESIS 9–11

FIRST DAY: Introduction

There is nothing quite as breathtaking as seeing a rainbow after a storm! These variegated prisms of color and light arch over the freshly washed landscape and remind us of God's covenant of mercy. After the great flood, God promised that He would never again destroy the whole world with a flood. He initiated a better plan to save His creation from corruption and judgment. Working through the lineage of Noah's son, Shem, God set apart one descendant after another to institute a godly line. It was through this chosen line that God ultimately provided the Messiah, His Son Jesus, to pay the penalty of judgment and free men from the corrupting influence of sin.

In Genesis 9 through 11, man's inevitable proclivity toward sin and rebellion is clearly portrayed. However, overarching this display of corruption is God's merciful covenant, and His unfolding plan to save His creation from the bondage of sin. In Romans 5:20, Paul declared the eternal truth that *where sin abounded, grace abounded much more.* Though man has a natural bent toward sin, God has provided the ultimate covenant of mercy to those who will receive Jesus as their Savior.

Ask God to help you embrace His overarching covenant of mercy.

SECOND DAY: Read Genesis 9:1–17

1. Having been saved from God's judgment by faith, Noah and his family were beginning a new chapter for the human race. After *God blessed Noah,* what did He instruct him to do? Genesis 9:1

   a. Compare this with Genesis 1:28a. What do you see?

2. God then established a different relationship between mankind and the animal kingdom. From Genesis 9:2–4 note and comment on the following ordinances of God concerning the animals:

   a. *Fear* of man (verse 2)

      (1) How is this a mercy?

   b. *Food* for man (verses 3–4)

      (1) Link this with Leviticus 17:11 and 14 to explain the significance of an animal's *blood.*

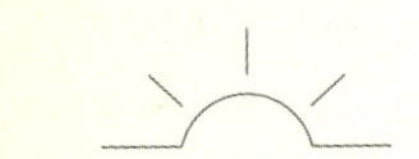

FOOD FOR THOUGHT

Before the flood, animals were not afraid of man. After the flood, God sanctioned animals as a source of food and caused them to have a fear and dread of man. According to Isaiah 11:6–9, Jesus will re-establish the original relationship between man and animals in the Kingdom Age.

3. In Genesis 9:5 God declared that He would *demand a reckoning* for murder, whether committed by man or animal. Record God's ordinance concerning this from Genesis 9:6.

   a. Pastor David Guzik points out, *Because man is made in the image of God, his life is inherently precious and cannot be taken without giving account to God.*[11] How does God's command help you to appreciate the sanctity of life?

4. God reiterated His command to *be fruitful and multiply.* He then established His *covenant* with all life on *earth* (Genesis 9:7–10). Cite this *covenant* from Genesis 9:11.

5. According to Genesis 9:12, God would give mankind a *sign of the covenant.* Use Genesis 9:13–17 to describe this *sign.*

   a. What does this reveal to you about God?

6. What most stands out to you about this new chapter in human history?

7. According to Genesis 9:14, God would accompany the *cloud* with a *rainbow*. When God looks at His rainbow, He remembers His covenant with you. What do you remember when you see a rainbow? Genesis 9:15–16

THIRD DAY: Read Genesis 9:18–29

1. From Genesis 9:18–19 summarize what you learn about *the sons of Noah.*

2. According to Genesis 9:20, Noah became a *farmer* and *planted a vineyard.* What happened when he *drank of the wine* from his vineyard? Genesis 9:21

    a. Though Noah was a great man of faith, he still sinned and made mistakes. How does this speak to you?

3. Read Genesis 9:22–23. Bible scholars say that Ham defiled his father in the tent. He then intentionally mocked his father to undermine his authority as a man of God. With this in mind, contrast Ham's sin with the actions of Shem and Japheth.

a. Connect this with the following Scriptures and share your thoughts:

(1) Exodus 20:12

(2) Proverbs 11:13

4. When Noah *awoke*, he *knew* what Ham *had done to him* (Genesis 9:24). Noah then prophesied concerning his sons. From Genesis 9:25–27 cite and remark on his prophecy concerning:

a. Ham's son Canaan (verses 25, 26b, 27b)

(1) Three times Noah declared that Canaan would be a *servant* to his brothers. According to the book of Joshua, this was the fate of the Canaanites when Israel conquered their land. What do you find interesting about this?

b. Shem (verse 26)

c. Japheth (verse 27)

FOOD FOR THOUGHT

Why was Canaan cursed? Bible scholars are divided on this point. Some say it was because the sins of Ham, the father, were inherited by his son, Canaan. Others say Canaan was complicit in his father's actions. A third opinion suggests that Canaan enjoyed hearing about Noah's humiliation.

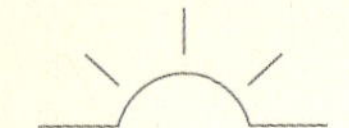

FOOD FOR THOUGHT

Noah was about 500 years old when his sons were born. According to the Bible time-lines, Noah, Shem, and Abraham would have all been living at the same time.

5. Genesis 9:28–29 records that Noah lived 350 years after the Flood and 950 years in total. Share any lessons you received from the testimony of Noah.

FOURTH DAY: Read Genesis 10

1. Genesis 10:1–32 documents the origins of the nations through the *genealogy of the sons of Noah.* We invite you to use the names listed below to find some of the nations originating from Noah's descendants:

FROM JAPHETH (verses 2–5): **Europe/Asia Minor**	**FROM HAM** (verses 6–20): **Egypt**	**FROM SHEM** (verses 21–31): **Middle East/ Arabian Peninsula**
Gomer	Cush	Elam
Magog	Mizraim	Asshur
Madai	Put (Phut)	Arphaxad
Javan	Canaan	Lud
Tubal	Havilah	Aram
Meshech	Raamah	Mash
Tiras	Sheba	Joktan
Ashkenaz	Dedan	Hazarmaveth
Riphath	Nimrod	Havilah
Togarmah	Ludim	Uzal
Elishah	Lehabim	Sheba
Tarshish	Pathrusim	Ophir
Kittim	Philistia (Philistines)	
	Caphtorim	
	Heth	

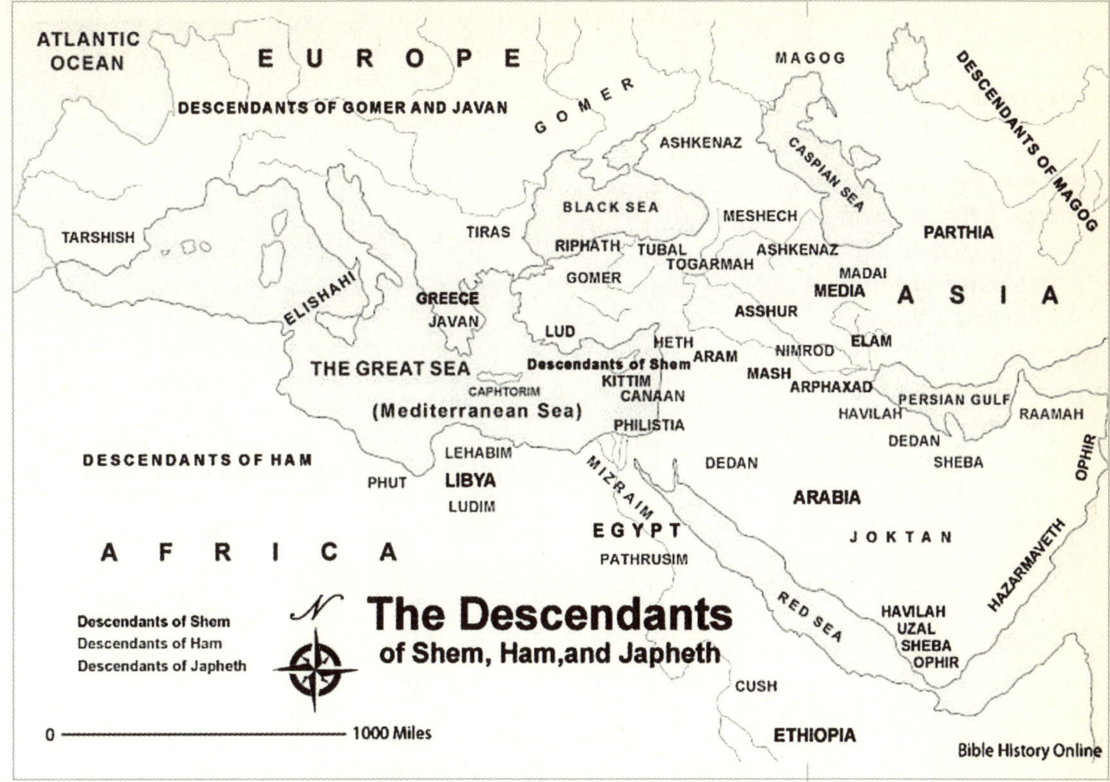

2. Genesis 10:8–12 highlights the legacy of Ham's grandson, Nimrod. Read these verses and record your observations concerning Nimrod.

   a. Bible scholars say that in context, the phrase *mighty hunter* indicates that Nimrod, whose name means *rebel,* was a hunter of men or a ruthless warrior in opposition to God. *The beginning of his kingdom was Babel,* later known as Babylon. This has been the site of many wicked and idolatrous kingdoms over the course of history, and will play a role in the end times (Revelation 18:1–4). What does this convey to you about the consequences of rebellion in a person's life?

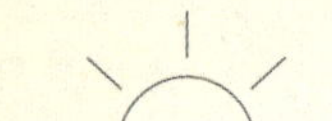

FOOD FOR THOUGHT

The name *Peleg* means *division*. Bible scholars say this could be a reference to either the continental divide when the land masses of the earth broke up, or to the events that unfolded in Genesis 11 concerning the Tower of Babel.

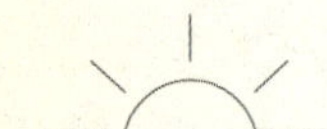

FOOD FOR THOUGHT

Of all those things here in the tenth chapter, there are no other documents that speak with the accuracy that Genesis does on the origin of the people groups and nations. You can't find any other piece of ancient literature that has this kind of accuracy.
—Pastor Brian Brodersen

(1) How is this a warning for you? See also 1 Samuel 15:23a.

(2) Why do you think Nimrod is mentioned in this chapter?

3. According to Genesis 10:25, what happened in the days of Peleg?

4. Compare the events of this chapter with the apostle Paul's declaration in Acts 17:26–27. What do you see?

FIFTH DAY: Read Genesis 11

1. Genesis 10:8–12 introduced Ham's grandson Nimrod, and Genesis 11 opened with the fate of his kingdom. Use Genesis 11:1–2 to set the scene for the building of this kingdom.

2. Contrary to God's command to *fill the earth* (Genesis 9:1), the people made their own plans. Use Genesis 11:3–4 to fill in their statements:

   a. *Come, let us* ______________________________ (verse 3)

   b. *Come, let us* ______________________________ (verse 4a)

   c. *Let us* ______________________________ (verse 4b)

   d. *Lest we be* ______________________________ (verse 4c)

      (1) Based on these statements, what do you think was their intention?

      (2) What dangers or sins can you identify in their plan?

3. According to Genesis 11:5, *the Lord came down to see the city and the tower* that the people of Shinar had built. Note and comment on:

   a. The problem (Genesis 11:6)

   b. God's intervention (Genesis 11:7)

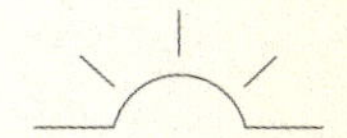

FOOD FOR THOUGHT

The building materials had the same waterproof substance that was used on the ark. Erecting a waterproof tower revealed the people's lack of trust in God's promise that He would never again flood the earth. They chose self-preservation over God's promise.

(1) Use Psalm 18:26 to understand how God deals with men.

(2) Remark on the contrast between God's *let Us* statement and the people's *let us* statements of Genesis 11:3–4.

c. The result (Genesis 11:8–9)

FOOD FOR THOUGHT

As Nimrod and his cohorts had held a council of conspiracy and aggression on earth, so God now called a "council," as it were, in heaven, to institute formal action to prevent the accomplishment of Nimrod's plans.[12]
—Dr. Henry Morris

(1) Notice that *the LORD scattered them abroad.* Contrast this with God's original intent (Genesis 9:1) and the people's intent in Genesis 11:4c. What do you see?

(2) *Babel* (Babylon) means *confusion.* Link this with Proverbs 16:5, 18 and James 3:16 and comment on the ultimate reason for the *confusion* at Babel.

(3) How do you see the attitude of Babel at work in the world today? See also Psalm 2:1–6.

(4) Pastor Warren Wiersbe says, *The unity of mankind would only give people a false sense of power that would lead them into even greater rebellion against God.*[13] How does this reveal the mercy of God in His judgment at Babel?

4. Genesis 11:10–26 listed the descendants of Shem, which became the primary focus of the biblical record. Genesis 11:27–32 introduced a key figure in this lineage, Abram. Read these verses and record anything you find interesting about Abram's background.

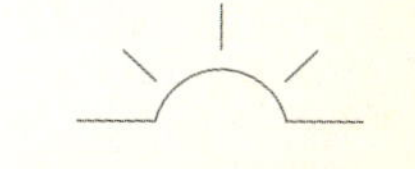

FOOD FOR THOUGHT

In the genealogy given after the flood, there is a marked decrease in the lifespan of mankind.

5. While man's plan was to join forces to become an all-powerful civilization at Babel, God's plan was to choose two ordinary people (Abram and Sarai) through whom He would accomplish His great purposes. How does this contrast minister to you?

SIXTH DAY: Review

1. Use your study this week in Genesis 9–11 to share your greatest takeaway concerning:

    a. Mankind and nature

    b. God's covenant

    c. Sanctity of life

    d. God's mercy

    e. The pervasive nature of sin

    f. Rebellion against God

    g. God's wisdom

2. Share any insights you received this week about Our Great Creator.

NOTES

NOTES

Abram's Call
GENESIS 12–14

FIRST DAY: Introduction

The life of faith is a life lived in response and obedience to God's Word. It is a life of adventure, promise, challenges, separation, victory, and divine encounters! It requires worship, sacrifice, waiting, and continually believing God's Word. This life begins when we hear and respond to God's call to us through Jesus. The Bible highlights Abram as a man of faith. As we study Abram's life, we see the practical and wondrous aspects of the life of faith. Like ours, Abram's life was filled with adventure, promise, challenges, separation, victory, and divine encounters.

Abram responded to God's call when he was seventy-five years old. He left his father's house, traveled some 450 miles, lived in a tent in a strange land, and was tested by famine, fear, separation, battles, successes, and delays. He is an example to us of what the life of faith experiences and entails.

Ask God to help you respond to His call and promises by faith.

SECOND DAY: Read Genesis 12:1–3

1. In Genesis 12 we are more fully introduced to Abram, who would become the father of the Jewish nation. Recall that Abram's family had left Ur *to go to the land of Canaan*, but settled in Haran (Genesis 11:31). Noting this, what had the Lord *said* to Abram? Genesis 12:1a

a. Read Joshua 24:2 to observe Abram's *family* background. How might this explain God's call to Abram to leave his *father's house*?

(1) Link this with Jesus' call to His disciples in Matthew 10:37–38. What do you see?

2. After God called Abram, He gave him powerful promises. Use Genesis 12:1b–3 to record and comment on God's *I will* promises:

a. Verse 1

b. Verse 2a

c. Verse 2b

d. Verse 3a

e. Verse 3b

3. God ended His call to Abram with a final promise of *blessing*. Comment on this promise as you connect it with its fulfillment in Galatians 3:8–9.

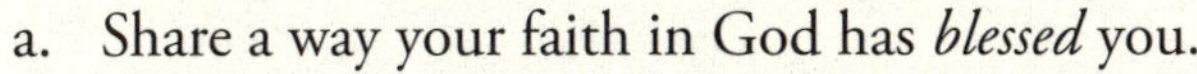

   a. Share a way your faith in God has *blessed* you.

4. From your study today, identify a present-day fulfillment of God's promises to Abram.

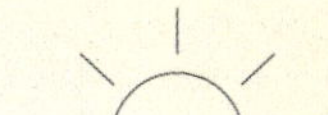

FOOD FOR THOUGHT

Barak is the Hebrew word meaning *to bless*. The extended meaning is *to do, or give something of value to another*. Five times in Genesis 12:2–3 this word is used to reveal God's intentions to Abram.

THIRD DAY: Read Genesis 12:4–20

1. After receiving God's command and promises, *Abram departed as the LORD had spoken to him* along with his wife, his nephew Lot, and *all their possessions*, and went to the land of Canaan (Genesis 12:4–6). Link this with Hebrews 11:8 to understand and comment on the magnitude of Abram's decision.

   a. How are you challenged by this aspect of faith?

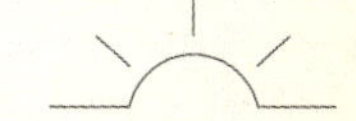

FOOD FOR THOUGHT

Wherever Abram went in the land of Canaan, he was marked by his tent and his altar. The tent marked him as a foreigner and nomad who did not belong to this world, and the altar marked him as a citizen of heaven who worshiped the true and living God.[14]
—Pastor Warren Wiersbe

2. What did God do after Abram obeyed His command? Genesis 12:7a

   a. How does this highlight the reward of obedience? See also John 14:21.

3. According to Genesis 12:7b–9, twice as Abram *journeyed* south, he *built an altar to the Lord*. Why do you think Abram did this?

4. When a *famine* came upon the land, *Abram went down to Egypt* (Genesis 12:10) where he felt threatened. Use Genesis 12:11–20 to briefly summarize and comment on:

   a. Abram's rationale (verses 11–13)

   b. The Egyptians' regard for Sarai (verses 14–16)

   c. God's response (verse 17)

   d. Pharaoh's rebuke (verses 18–20)

FOOD FOR THOUGHT

Note that Abram's faith was still developing. God was patient and gracious to Abram and used Abram's folly in Egypt to show him the faithfulness of His covenant.

(1) What evidence do you detect of God's grace to Abram in Egypt?

5. Share a way God's grace has covered your mistakes.

FOURTH DAY: Read Genesis 13

1. After Abram's time in Egypt, he returned to Canaan. From Genesis 13:1–2 describe Abram's entourage and possessions at this time.

2. Use Genesis 13:3–4 to note and comment on the significance of Bethel.

3. According to Genesis 13:5, Lot also had *flocks and herds and tents,* which resulted in conflict. Use Genesis 13:6–13 to identify and remark on:

   a. The dilemma (verses 6–7)

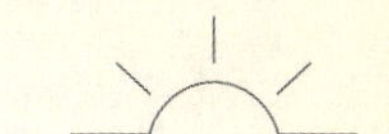

FOOD FOR THOUGHT

In the Bible, Egypt is a symbol of the world and bondage. Notice that Abram did not build an altar or call on the name of the LORD while he was in Egypt.

b. Abram's solution (verses 8–9)

(1) Abram was older than Lot and had been promised the land by God. Why does this make Abram's solution so gracious?

(2) Strife is defined as *disputes, quarrels, and contentions*. How is Abram's response to *strife* an example to you? See also Romans 12:10 and Philippians 2:4.

c. Lot's choice (verses 10–11a)

d. The outcome (verses 11b–13)

(1) What does Lot's choice suggest to you about him?

4. *After Lot had separated from him*, the Lord spoke to Abram (Genesis 13:14a). Use Genesis 13:14b–17 to answer the following:

a. What did God tell Abram to do? (verses 14b, 17)

b. How did God expand the promise given to Abram in Genesis 12:2–3? (verses 15–16)

(1) Considering Abram's age and Sarai's barrenness, why would this promise require faith?

(2) Why do you think these promises would encourage Abram after separating from Lot?

5. Abram then *moved his tent* and *dwelt* in Hebron. Remark on what he did there. Genesis 13:18

6. Use Hebrews 11:8–10 to share a way Abram's faith motivates you.

FIFTH DAY: Read Genesis 14

1. Genesis 14:1–10 recounts a war between various kings of the city-states around Canaan. Use these verses to briefly summarize this war.

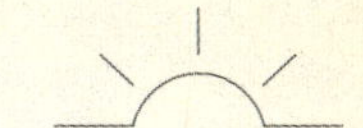

FOOD FOR THOUGHT

The LORD's promise to give the land of Canaan to Abram's offspring is the single most repeated affirmation in the Torah. At least thirty-seven references are made to it in the books of Moses.[15]
—HCSB Study Bible

2. When the kings of Sodom and Gomorrah were overthrown in battle, what did the conquering armies take from these cities? Genesis 14:11–12

   a. *One who had escaped came and told Abram* what had happened (Genesis 14:13). According to Genesis 14:14–16, how did Abram respond when he *heard* this news?

      (1) Considering Lot's behavior up to this point, what does this convey to you about Abram?

3. After Abram's victory and meeting with the king of Sodom (Genesis 14:17), he encountered an intriguing figure—Melchizedek. According to Genesis 14:18–20:

   a. Who was Melchizedek? (verse 18)

      (1) From Psalm 110:4, read the Messianic prophecy that was written 900 years after this encounter. Without the explanation given in Hebrews 7:1–3, the significance of this encounter would have remained mysterious. Use Hebrews 7:1–3 to unlock this mystery.

b. What did Melchizedek do? (verses 18–19a)

(1) From 1 Corinthians 11:23–26, remark on the symbolism of the *bread and wine.*

(2) Notice that Melchizedek *blessed* Abram. Use Hebrews 7:7 to explain why this is significant.

c. What did Melchizedek declare? (verses 19b–20a)

(1) How might this have encouraged Abram?

d. What did Melchizedek receive from Abram? (verse 20b)

(1) Link this with Hebrews 7:4 and share your thoughts.

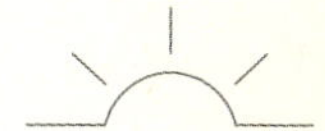

FOOD FOR THOUGHT

Biblically, a *tithe* was one-tenth of income. This was the first act of tithing recorded in the Bible. It anticipated the tithe that God would require (Malachi 3:10).

4. In Genesis 14:21 the *king of Sodom* made Abram the tempting offer of all *the goods* from the battle. In your own words, express Abram's response to the king of Sodom. Genesis 14:22–24

    a. What impresses you about Abram's response?

5. From today's study, what is your greatest takeaway about Abram's faith?

SIXTH DAY: Review

1. Use your study this week from Genesis 12–14 to reflect on the life of Abram concerning:

    a. God's call

    b. Abram's obedience

    c. Abram's worship

d. Abram's challenge

e. Abram's faith

f. Abram's choices

g. God's blessings

2. Genesis 12–14 records four instances in which Abram built an altar to the Lord. Oswald Chambers pointed out, *Commentators notice one interesting point in Abraham's life, whenever he neglected to erect an altar, he went astray.*[16] What does this convey about worship?

3. What stands out to you most about Abram's relationship to Our Great Creator?

NOTES

The Covenant
GENESIS 15–17

FIRST DAY: Introduction

God's promises and covenants do not depend upon our strengths, schemes, and strivings. When we try to make God's will happen, we employ our feeble nature, our fallible plans, and our finite understanding. This is why our attempts fail so miserably. God knows the perfect time, way, and place to accomplish His will. He requires only our faith and cooperation through obedience.

Through Abram's example we see the problems that are created when we try to preempt God in fulfilling His promises. God made a covenant with Abram to bless him, give him understanding, and bless all the nations through his seed. God made it clear to Abram, through a covenant ritual, that He Himself was responsible to fulfill His Word. When Abram looked at the difficulties and impossibilities of God's plan, he conspired with Sarai to accomplish God's will through his own human efforts. Their plan brought about unforeseen and disastrous problems. However, God in His great grace did not discard His promises to Abram. Instead God reiterated and clarified the work that He alone would and could do.

Are you discouraged by the obstacles to God's promises in your life? Are you tempted to preempt God's plans with your own schemes? Stop! Learn a lesson from Abram's life about how to lean into God and trust Him to fulfill His Word to you.

Ask God to increase your confidence in His ability to fulfill His word to you.

SECOND DAY: Read Genesis 15:1–7

1. Some time after Abram's military victory against a conglomeration of kings and his refusal to take the spoils from the king of Sodom, *the LORD came to him in a vision.* What did the Lord say to Abram? Genesis 15:1

    a. Considering the events of Abram's life, why was this word so needed?

    b. How does this word speak to you?

FOOD FOR THOUGHT

This is the first time in Scripture that God said, *Do not be afraid.* This same instruction is repeated some 365 times. It is the most repeated command in the Bible.

2. Although this word was reassuring, Abram was concerned about God's promise regarding his descendants, because he was still *childless* and his only *heir* was his servant Eliezer (Genesis 15:2–3). God answered Abram's concern by expounding on His promises. From Genesis 15:4–7 note and comment on the *word of the LORD* concerning:

    a. Abram's *heir* (verse 4)

    b. Abram's *descendants* (verse 5)

c. The *land* (verse 7)

(1) Record Abram's response to these promises from verse 6.

(2) This principle of *justification by faith* is so essential, it was reiterated throughout the New Testament. Link Abram's faith with these Scriptures and remark on this:

(a) Romans 4:3, 5

(b) Romans 4:20–24

(c) Galatians 3:6–7, 9

(d) James 2:23

(3) In Hebrew, the phrase *he believed in the Lord* indicates that Abram put his full weight on God. Share an area of your life in which you desire to follow Abram's example.

3. From your study today, share something that ministered to you concerning:

   a. God's interaction with Abram

   b. Abram's response to God

   c. Your faith being accounted to you for righteousness

FOOD FOR THOUGHT

Biblically, a covenant is defined as a *binding agreement of loyalty and fidelity between two or more parties.*

THIRD DAY: Read Genesis 15:8–21

1. Abram asked for confirmation when God promised him the land (Genesis 15:8). God answered by telling Abram to prepare for a covenant. Use Genesis 15:9–11 to describe how this was done.

2. *When the sun was going down*, Abram fell asleep, and *horror and great darkness fell upon him* (Genesis 15:12). This preceded God's word to Abram about the future of his descendants. Summarize and remark on this word from Genesis 15:13–16, 18b–21 concerning:

   a. Abram's descendants (verses 13, 14b, 16, 18)

b. The nation his descendants would serve (verse 14a)

c. Abram's future (verse 15)

d. The Amorites (verse 16)

(1) Notice God's statement that *the iniquity of the Amorites is not yet complete* (verse 16). This indicates that God would give them another 400 years before He judged their sin. Link this with 2 Peter 3:9 and share your thoughts.

3. After these declarations, what did God do? Genesis 15:17–18a

a. In an ancient *covenant* such as this, the animals would be cut in half. Then **both** parties, coming from opposite ends, would meet in the middle, having passed *between* the pieces. By doing this, they were essentially stating that if either of them broke *covenant* they would deserve the fate of these animals. Why is it significant, then, that only God passed all the way through between the animals?

(1) How did God's actions ratify the certainty of the covenant He made with Abram?

4. Link this covenant with Hebrews 9:15 and share your heart concerning the new *covenant* you have through Jesus Christ.

FOURTH DAY: Read Genesis 16

1. Although God had given Abram promises concerning his descendants, *Sarai, Abram's wife, had borne him no children.* Summarize Sarai's solution to this problem from Genesis 16:1–4a.

   a. What do you think prompted Sarai to come up with such a plan?

   b. Why do you think *Abram heeded the voice of Sarai* in this matter?

c. Observe that Abram had been in Canaan *ten years* at this point and was now about 85 years old. Although bearing a child through a concubine was a typical practice in this culture, according to Genesis 16:4, what resulted from copying the cultural solution?

(1) How is this a warning for you? See Proverbs 3:5–6.

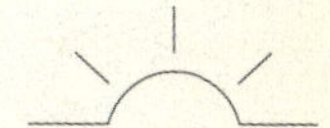

FOOD FOR THOUGHT

Note that the mention of God is absent in the first six verses of this chapter. He was also absent from the verses that described Abram's previous decision to travel to Egypt during a famine (Genesis 12:10-16).

2. When Hagar *conceived*, she began to despise Sarai (Genesis 16:4b). As a result, Sarai told Abram, *This is all your fault! I put my servant into your arms, but now that she's pregnant she treats me with contempt. The LORD will show who's wrong—you or me!* (Genesis 16:5 NLT). What did Sarai do next? Genesis 16:6

a. What do you think of Sarai's actions?

b. How did Hagar respond to Sarai's treatment?

(1) How might this complicated situation have been averted?

3. The *Angel of the* LORD came to Hagar in the *wilderness* and began to speak with her (Genesis 16:7–8). Use Genesis 16:9–12 to note and comment on:
   a. The Lord's command (verse 9)

   b. The Lord's promise (verse 10)

   c. The Lord's word concerning Hagar's son (verses 11–12)

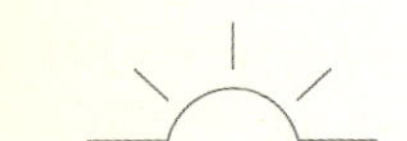

FOOD FOR THOUGHT

The name *Ishmael* means *God hears.*

      (1) How do you see the Lord's mercy even in this situation?

4. Remark on Hagar's response to God's word from Genesis 16:13–14.

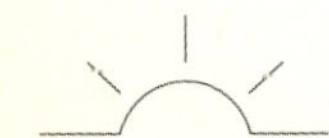

FOOD FOR THOUGHT

The Angel of the LORD appeared fifty times in the Old Testament and is mentioned first in Genesis 16:9. Bible scholars widely believe that in times past, Jesus appeared to people in human form as *the Angel of the* LORD.

   a. What does it mean to you that God is *The God Who Sees*?

5. Hagar returned and *bore Abram a son* when he was eighty-six years old (Genesis 16:15–16). What do you find noteworthy about her decision to return?

6. Drawing from your lesson today, why do you think it is folly to involve human schemes in an attempt to fulfill God's promises?

FIFTH DAY: Read Genesis 17

1. Thirteen years after the birth of Ishmael, God again *appeared to Abram*. Use Genesis 17:1–8 to cite the following:

   a. God's self-identification (verse 1a)

      (1) This name in Hebrew is *El Shaddai*, meaning *all-sufficient, all-powerful God*; it is the first instance in which God identified Himself by this name. Why do you think God revealed Himself to Abram in this way?

   b. God's command (verse 1b)

      (1) The word *blameless* means *single-hearted, sincere, wholly devoted to the Lord*. Why do you think God required this?

   c. God's *covenant* (verses 2–8)

(1) The name *Abram* means *exalted father*, while *Abraham* means *father of a multitude*. Considering Abram's condition, why was this remarkable?

(2) Notice in verse 5 that God said He had made Abram *a father of many nations* **before** he had a legitimate son. Link this with Romans 4:17b and share your thoughts.

2. In Genesis 17:9–14 God commanded Abraham and his household to be circumcised. Note that God made His covenant with Abraham before he was circumcised. Circumcision, thus, became an outward indication of a covenant that was already established. Link this passage with Deuteronomy 30:6 and Colossians 2:11 to explain the true significance of circumcision.

   a. Why do you think God required this before the promise could be fulfilled?

3. In Genesis 17:15–16 what did God tell Abraham about his *wife* Sarai?

a. Remember, at one point Sarah thought God's promises did not include her. Now God made a special mention of Sarah's part in His covenant with Abraham. How does this minister to you about your inclusion in God's promises?

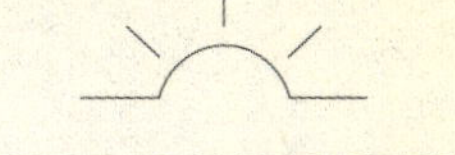

FOOD FOR THOUGHT

Sarai and *Sarah* both mean *princess*. Bible teachers often point out that God removed the *"i"* from Sarai's name and inserted *"yah,"* a form of His own name.

4. Read Genesis 17:17–21 and remark on:

 a. Abraham's response to God's word concerning Sarah (verses 17–18)

 b. God's covenant to Abraham (verse 19)

 c. God's promise concerning Ishmael (verse 20)

 d. Isaac (verse 21)

5. After God *finished talking* with Abraham (Genesis 17:22), he immediately acted on God's instructions. What does this convey to you? Genesis 17:23–27

6. In Genesis 17 God used the word *covenant* thirteen times and promised *I will* thirteen times. What does this reveal to you about God?

SIXTH DAY: Review

1. From your study this week in Genesis 15–17, use the following chart to highlight the progression of God's promises to Abraham concerning:

The Land	Genesis 15:7	Genesis 15:13–21	Genesis 17:8
His Descendants	Genesis 15:4–5	Genesis 17:4–7	Genesis 17:15–16, 19–21

a. Why do you think God repeated His promises?

2. Record a promise you have received from Our Great Creator.

3. Share a way you saw God's grace demonstrated toward:

   a. Abraham

   b. Sarah

   c. Hagar

   d. Ishmael

NOTES

Intercession
GENESIS 18–19

FIRST DAY: Introduction

More often than not, we are unaware of the jeopardy, danger, and troubles that threaten to disrupt our lives. Thank God that Jesus, knowing all things, intercedes for us before the throne of God (Romans 8:34, Hebrews 7:25). Even as Jesus intercedes on our behalf, we are to pray and intercede for others that they might be saved from wrath and become recipients of God's promises.

Through Abraham's example we see the work of intercession. Abraham welcomed the Lord into his home. He fellowshipped with the Lord and received His promises. God then revealed His plan to Abraham concerning the wicked cities of Sodom and Gomorrah. Immediately, Abraham recognized the jeopardy of his nephew Lot and began to call upon God's character to spare the righteous. Abraham's prayer availed! In Genesis 19 we see the results of Abraham's intercession for the unwilling participant—Lot. Even though Lot was hesitant to acknowledge his jeopardy and to cooperate with the angels, he was delivered because of Abraham's prayers.

We have the same power, through prayer, to intercede even for the uncooperative and defiled. As we welcome God into our lives, fellowship with Him, and embrace His promises, we receive revelation concerning the jeopardy of the world. Our response is to pray, calling on God's righteous character and grace to save and deliver. God hears and works through our prayers in divine ways to bring salvation even to the hesitant and uncooperative. This is why *men always ought to pray and not lose heart* (Luke 18:1).

Ask God to reveal to you the powerful effect you have through prayer.

SECOND DAY: Read Genesis 18:1–15

1. God *appeared* to Abraham soon after He established His covenant with him. Read about this encounter in Genesis 18:1–8 and cite Abraham's:

   a. Haste

   b. Hospitality

      (1) Link Abraham's actions with Hebrews 13:2. What do you see?

FOOD FOR THOUGHT

In the text of Genesis 18:3, the Hebrew word for *Lord* is *Adonay*—a word reserved for God. *Adonay* is the emphatic term for *Lord*. We don't know whether Abraham knew his visitors' identity at the outset, but by the story's end, Abraham certainly knew he had been talking with God.[17]
—NLT Study Bible

2. As they ate, the men asked Abraham where Sarah was, and he told them she was *in the tent* (Genesis 18:9). What promise did the Lord make concerning her? Genesis 18:10a

3. According to Genesis 18:10b, *Sarah was listening in the tent door*. From Genesis 18:12, remark on her reaction to this proclamation.

   a. Use Genesis 18:11 to explain why she reacted this way.

4. The Lord heard Sarah *laugh*, yet He reiterated His promise concerning her (Genesis 18:13–14). From Genesis 18:14a, fill in the blanks with His penetrating rhetorical question:

Is ____________ too________for the _________?

a. Connect this with the following Scriptures, noting what most ministers to you:

(1) Job 42:2

(2) Jeremiah 32:17

(3) Luke 1:37

(4) Ephesians 3:20

(a) Share an area of your life in which you need to consider this truth.

5. Sarah *denied* laughing, even though God affirmed that she did (Genesis 18:15). In spite of Sarah's apparent unbelief, what did God say about her in Hebrews 11:11?

   a. Why do you think God reaffirmed His promise within earshot of Sarah?

      (1) How does this minister to you?

THIRD DAY: Read Genesis 18:16–33

1. After their meal, the men headed toward Sodom and Abraham went *to send them on their way*. Then the Lord spoke of His plans, indicating that He would not *hide from Abraham* what He was doing (Genesis 18:16–17). Link this with Amos 3:7 and share your thoughts.

2. From Genesis 18:18–19, note and comment on what the Lord said concerning:

   a. His plans for Abraham (verse 18)

   b. His purpose for Abraham (verse 19)

(1) In the Hebrew, when God said He had *known* Abraham, it meant that He cared for and chose him. Link this with Jesus' words in John 10:14. How does this encourage you?

3. God then declared His intentions concerning Sodom and Gomorrah. From Genesis 18:20–21, describe the *outcry* that came to God's attention and His response.

   a. Use the following verses to ascertain why an *outcry* arose *against Sodom and Gomorrah*:

      (1) Isaiah 3:9

      (2) Jeremiah 23:14

      (3) Ezekiel 16:49–50

4. When *the men* left for Sodom, *Abraham still stood before the Lord* to intercede on its behalf (Genesis 18:22). Use your own words to record the three questions he asked God:

   a. Genesis 18:23

b. Genesis 18:24

c. Genesis 18:25

(1) Abraham was not questioning God's justice, but pleading with Him based on what he knew of His character. From Abraham's dialogue with God, what do you recognize about God's character? See also Ezekiel 33:11.

FOOD FOR THOUGHT

There are three important principles observed from this dialogue:
1. God is not hasty to bring judgment on any city or person.
2. Even a tiny minority may have a remarkable influence for good.
3. Abraham's prayer was persistent yet extremely reverent.

5. Abraham began to intercede to the Lord on behalf of the *righteous* in Sodom. Use Genesis 18:24–33 to briefly comment on the progression of his intercession.

a. What most stands out to you from Abraham's interaction with the Lord?

b. Pastor David Guzik says, *This is the kind of heart God wanted to draw out of Abraham—a heart that cared so much for people made in the image of God that he worked hard to intercede on behalf of a city that deserved judgment.*[18] How does this deepen your understanding of intercession and its purpose?

c. What lesson do you receive concerning:

(1) Intercession (See also James 5:16)

(2) God's character (See also 2 Peter 3:9)

6. James 2:23b says Abraham *was called the friend of God.* How do you see this evidenced in your study today?

a. Link this with John 15:15. Why are you blessed to be called a *friend of God*?

FOURTH DAY: Read Genesis 19:1–14

1. Recall from Genesis 13:12 that Lot was *living as far as Sodom,* then living *in Sodom* (Genesis 14:12), and finally *sitting in the gate* (Genesis 19:1) where the *two angels* found him. This indicates that Lot had become a prominent political figure and judge in Sodom. What do you find interesting about this digression? See Psalm 1:1.

2. From Genesis 19:1b–3, summarize and remark on Lot's interaction with the *angels.*

3. *Before they lay down* for the night, a disturbing incident occurred. Use Genesis 19:4–11 to note and comment on:

   a. The demands of the men of Sodom (verses 4–5, 9)

      (1) Notice that these men accused Lot of *acting as a judge* over them. What does this convey about Lot's interaction with them? See also 2 Peter 2:7–8.

   b. The response of Lot (verses 6–8)

      (1) What does this response indicate about Lot's perspective?

   c. The actions of the angels (verses 10–11)

4. From Genesis 19:12–13 cite the warning and instruction of the angels.

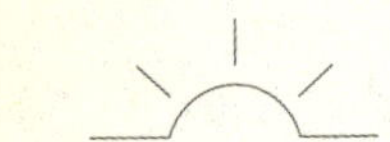

FOOD FOR THOUGHT

Jesus is the One who elevated and honored women. Through Christianity, women have been able to rise and take their proper place, not as subservient or in any way subservient to men, but rather on an equal basis with men. But you won't find that in any culture outside of where the Christian gospel has gone.[19]
—Pastor Chuck Smith

a. After hearing this, Lot warned his *sons-in-law* of the impending judgment. Use Genesis 19:14 to remark on their response.

(1) What does this response reveal about Lot's witness among his family?

5. Lot was a man who had allowed himself to be greatly influenced by his culture. How does your study today caution you concerning the effects of a compromised life?

FIFTH DAY: Read Genesis 19:15–38

1. In spite of Lot's pleas, his *sons-in-law* disregarded his warning of impending judgment. *When the morning dawned*, it was time for Lot to flee from Sodom. From Genesis 19:15–22, summarize Lot's deliverance, highlighting the following:

   a. The urgency of the *angels* (verses 15–17, 22)

   b. Lot's hesitation (verse 16)

   c. Lot's bargaining (verses 18–21)

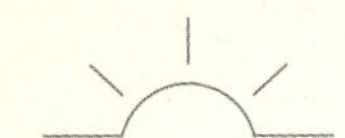

FOOD FOR THOUGHT

The first time God rescued Lot, he was a prisoner of war (Genesis 14:12, 16), *and he went right back to Sodom. That painful experience should have warned him that he was out of the will of God .... Now God had to take Lot by the hand and forcibly drag him out of Sodom.*[20]
—Pastor Warren Wiersbe

(1) In what way was God *merciful* to Lot?

2. When *the sun had risen*, Lot finally entered the city of Zoar, which means *small* or *insignificant* (Genesis 19:23). What happened as soon as Lot was safe? Genesis 19:24–25

   a. Pastor Chuck said of Lot's wife (Genesis 19:26), *The phrase "looked back" can be translated "turned back." Lot's wife actually began to turn back toward Sodom and in turning back towards Sodom, she was caught in the great conflagration and the bubbling, boiling, spewing salts covered her.*[21] Link this with Luke 17:32–33 and share your thoughts.

3. *Early in the morning*, Abraham went and *looked toward Sodom and Gomorrah* (Genesis 19:27–28a). From Genesis 19:28b describe what he saw.

   a. According to Genesis 19:29, why was Lot *sent out* by God?

(1) What does this reveal to you about intercession?

4. Even as Lot was being delivered from Sodom, he was negotiating with the angels about his next destination. After he left Zoar he went to an isolated place of his own choosing and *dwelt in the mountains* with his two daughters (Genesis 19:30). Use Genesis 19:31–38 to briefly summarize the grievous events that took place because of Lot's choices.

   a. The Moabites and Ammonites became enemies of Abraham's descendants in later generations. How does this underscore the far-reaching effects of Lot's compromise?

5. Pastor J. Vernon McGee says, *There is many a man today who may be a saved man, but due to his lifestyle or where he lives, he loses his family, his influence, and his testimony.*[22] Connect this with 1 Corinthians 3:15 and record your summation of Lot's life.

6. How is Lot's life a cautionary warning to you?

SIXTH DAY: Review

1. From your study this week, share something that spoke to you concerning:

    a. God's promises

    b. Intercession

    c. Compromise

    d. Judgment

    e. Mercy

2. What insights did you receive in Genesis 18 and 19 about Our Great Creator?

NOTES

NOTES

A Promise Fulfilled

GENESIS 20–21

FIRST DAY: Introduction

God is determined to fulfill His word to us! However, we often hinder, delay, and even jeopardize God's promises by our self-will, self-effort, and attempts at self-preservation. God is not looking for perfect people or perfect faith. God is, however, seeking to perfect our faith in order that He might fulfill His promises to us.

Abraham was not a perfect man, nor did he have perfect faith. He had observable lapses of faith in God's promise when:

- He went to Egypt and released Sarah to Pharaoh's harem
- He sired a child with the Egyptian maid, Hagar
- He again released Sarah, this time to Abimelech's harem

Yet, in spite of Abraham's follies, God still worked to:

- Protect his honor
- Preserve his life
- Mature his faith
- Fulfill His promise to him

In God's perfect time, will, and way, Abraham received God's promise.

Ask God to perfect your faith.

SECOND DAY: Read Genesis 20

1. According to Genesis 20:1–2, Abraham and Sarah *journeyed* south and came to Gerar, where Abimelech was king. Compare this with Genesis 12:10–15 to record and remark on what occurred once again.

2. As in the past, Abraham's fear-based decision had consequences, yet God protected His promise. Use Genesis 20:3–16 to note and comment on the following:

   a. God's interaction with Abimelech (verses 3–7)

      (1) Notice God called Abraham a *prophet.* One aspect of a prophet's ministry was to intercede on behalf of others. How do you see Abraham fulfilling this role? See also Genesis 18:19.

   b. Abimelech's confrontation with Abraham (verses 8–10)

   c. Abraham's excuse (verses 11–13)

      (1) Use Proverbs 29:25 to identify and remark on the flaws in Abraham's excuse.

d. Abimelech's actions (verses 14–16)

(1) Abraham thought there was no *fear of God* in Gerar. How do Abimelech's actions prove otherwise?

3. What happened when Abraham *prayed* for Abimelech and his household? Genesis 20:17–18

a. What evidence of God's mercy do you find in this situation?

4. Considering this entire confrontation, share any insights you received concerning:

a. God

b. Abimelech

c. Abraham

THIRD DAY: Read Genesis 21:1–7

1. In Genesis 21:1 God turned His attention to Sarah. Use this verse to fill in the blanks below:

   And the L*ORD visited Sarah* ____ _____ ______ ________,

   and the L*ORD did for Sarah* ____ _____ ______ ________.

   a. Link this with the following Scriptures and share what ministers to you:

      (1) Numbers 23:19

      (2) Habakkuk 2:3

      (3) Hebrews 10:23

   b. Twenty-five years had passed since God's original promise to Abraham and Sarah. Yet, according to Genesis 21:2, Sarah *bore Abraham a son* at the *set time* which God had promised. How does this speak to you concerning:

      (1) God's promises

      (2) God's faithfulness

(3) God's timing

(4) The need for patience

2. Use Genesis 21:3–7 to capture the joy and wonder of this miraculous birth.

   a. The name *Isaac* means *laughter*. Why was this a fitting name?

   b. What further insight about this birth do you find in Hebrews 11:11?

3. Read Hebrews 6:12 and ask God to reveal an area in which you need *faith and patience* in order to receive God's promise to you.

FOURTH DAY: Read Genesis 21:8–21

1. According to Genesis 21:8, once Isaac was *weaned*, Abraham held a *great feast* to celebrate. What did Sarah witness at this *feast*? Genesis 21:9

   a. *Therefore*, what did Sarah tell Abraham to do? Genesis 21:10

      (1) Comment on Abraham's reaction to Sarah's concerns. Genesis 21:11

2. Use Genesis 21:12–13 to remark on God's word concerning:

   a. Sarah

      (1) It is important to realize that Ishmael was a young man, and according to the Hebrew word (*tsachaq*) was mocking and making sport of Isaac (Galatians 4:29). How does this justify Sarah's concern?

   b. Isaac (verse 12b)

   c. Ishmael (verses 12a, 13)

(1) In the New Testament, we see that this conflict between Isaac and Ishmael has a spiritual application. The apostle Paul compared Hagar and Ishmael with the bondage of the life of the flesh, and Sarah and Isaac with the freedom of the spiritual life in Christ. With this in mind, read Galatians 4:22–31 to write your observations concerning:

(a) The son of Hagar—the *bondwoman*

(b) The son of Sarah—the *freewoman*

(c) What does this convey to you concerning the necessity for us, as believers, to *cast out* the life of the flesh?

3. Of his own volition, Abraham *rose early* and sent Hagar and Ishmael away with provisions (Genesis 21:14a). Use Genesis 21:14b–16 to capture Hagar's desperate plight as she *wandered* in the wilderness.

   a. *God heard the voice of the lad* and *called* out to Hagar. From Genesis 21:17–18, note and comment on what He told her.

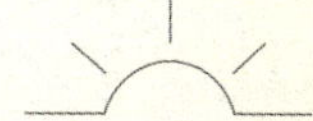

FOOD FOR THOUGHT

Nowhere do we read that Ishmael caused great joy in Abraham's home. From before his birth, Ishmael was a source of painful trouble, and after he matured, he caused even greater conflict. The old nature is not able to produce the fruit of the Spirit, no matter how hard it tries.

4. Describe God's miraculous provision for Hagar and Ishmael from Genesis 21:19.

   a. How does God's care for Hagar and Ishmael minister to you?

5. Use Genesis 21:20–21 to summarize the life of Ishmael.

   a. Ishmael became the father of the Arab nations. Link this with the prophecy concerning his future in Genesis 16:11–12, and share a way you see this prophetic word in effect today.

6. From your study today, share something that stands out to you concerning:

   a. God's will

   b. God's compassion

FIFTH DAY: Read Genesis 21:22–34

1. At this time, Abraham was still living in Abimelech's kingdom. In Genesis 21:22a Abimelech and his military *commander* came to Abraham. According to Genesis 21:22b–23, what did they:

   a. Acknowledge (verse 22b)

   b. Request (verse 23)

      (1) What does this reveal to you about Abraham's witness among them?

      (2) What witness do you desire to have?

2. Abraham swore to deal well with Abimelech (Genesis 21:24). However, why did he also rebuke Abimelech? Genesis 21:25

3. Abimelech claimed he did not *know* his *servants* had done this (Genesis 21:26). How did the men resolve this conflict? Genesis 21:27–31

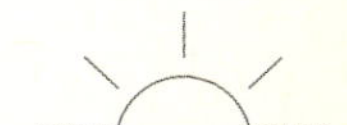

FOOD FOR THOUGHT

Beersheba means *Well of the Oath* or *Well of the Seven.* The word *to swear* in Hebrew means *to bind by seven things.*

4. After making a *covenant at Beersheba*, the men parted ways (Genesis 21:32). What did Abraham do after this? Genesis 21:33–34

   a. Abraham already knew God as *El-Elyon* (*God Most High*, Genesis 14:18,22) and *El-Shaddai* (*The All-Sufficient One*, Genesis 17:1). Yet, this was the first time he used the name *the LORD, the Everlasting God*, translated *El-Olam* (Genesis 21:33). What does this suggest to you concerning Abraham's faith?

      (1) These names of God represent aspects of His character and nature. Which name of God ministers to you presently?

FOOD FOR THOUGHT

The tamarisk tree grows 20–30 feet high and is evergreen. By planting this tree, Abraham was creating a legacy and staking his legal claim to be in Beersheba.

SIXTH DAY: Review

1. The focal point of our study this week was the long-awaited fulfillment of God's promise. Significantly, there are many parallels between the birth of Isaac and the birth of Jesus. Fill in the chart to explore some of these remarkable comparisons:

	ISAAC	JESUS	YOUR TAKEAWAY
The Promise	Genesis 17:17, 19	Isaiah 7:14	
The Impossibility	Genesis 18:13–14	Luke 1:34–35, 37	
The Timing	Genesis 21:1	Galatians 4:4	
The Miracle	Genesis 21:2, 7	Matthew 1:20–23; Luke 2:7	
The Joy	Genesis 21:6	Luke 1:46–47	

2. How are you blessed by the fact that Our Great Creator makes promises to us that *He* fulfills?

NOTES

The Sacrifice
GENESIS 22–23

FIRST DAY: Introduction

The Old Testament events, laws, rituals, history, and poetry can only be understood through the lens of Jesus Christ:

- *Then I said, "Behold, I come; in the scroll of the book it is written of Me."* Psalm 40:7
- *And beginning at Moses and all the Prophets, He expounded to them in all the Scriptures the things concerning Himself.* Luke 24:27
- *You search the Scriptures, for in them you think you have eternal life; and these are they which testify of Me.* John 5:39
- *Then I said, "Behold, I have come—in the volume of the book it is written of Me—to do Your will, O God."* Hebrews 10:7

When Jesus is placed in the volume of the book, the wisdom, majesty, and compassion of God is realized and everything makes sense.

Without Jesus, God's testing of Abraham (to sacrifice his beloved son) seems cruel and arbitrary. However, when Jesus is inserted into the story, Abraham's sacrifice becomes a foreshadowing of God's own sacrifice. The story then comes alive with deep truths, tender compassions, and amazing insights.

The Old Testament can appear arbitrary, harsh, and inexplicable without Jesus at its center. In the same way, your life can seem arbitrary, harsh, and inexplicable until you place Jesus at the center. When Jesus is given center place, He infuses divine purpose, mercy, and compassion into every part of our lives.

Ask God to illuminate your life through the lens of Jesus Christ.

SECOND DAY: Read Genesis 22:1–8

1. Genesis 22:1 begins, *Now it came to pass after these things. These things* referred to the long-awaited birth of Isaac (through Sarah), who was by now a young man and the heir to all God's promises. It was at this time *God tested Abraham*. The Hebrew word for *tested* is *nissah,* which means *to prove the value of.* What does this indicate to you about God's plans for Abraham and his son, Isaac?

   a. How did Abraham respond to God's call? Genesis 22:1b

      (1) What does this convey to you about Abraham?

   b. Link this event with 1 Peter 1:6–7. What do you see?

2. Use Genesis 22:2 to note and comment on:

   a. God's description of Isaac (verse 2a)

   b. God's command concerning Isaac (verse 2b)

(1) Pastor Warren Wiersbe points out, *Isaac was Abraham's only son, and the future of the covenant rested in him. Isaac was a miracle child, the gift of God to Abraham and Sarah in response to their faith. Abraham and Sarah loved Isaac very much and had built their whole future around him.*[23] How does this magnify the seriousness of Abraham's test of faith?

c. This is the first mention of love in the Bible; significantly, it is the love of a father for his son. This also foreshadowed the sacrifice of Jesus for our sins. Link this with Luke 3:22 and John 3:16 and share your thoughts.

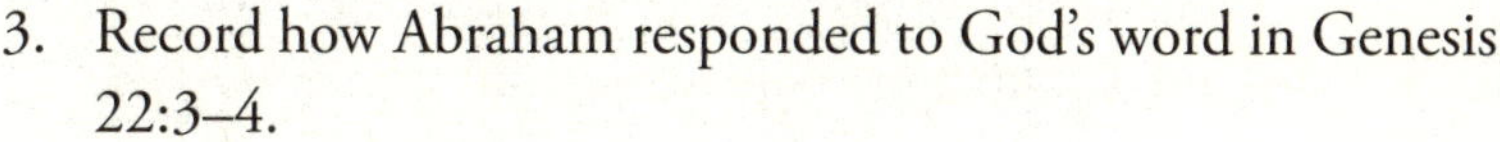

3. Record how Abraham responded to God's word in Genesis 22:3–4.

a. Connect the length of Abraham's journey (verse 4) with Matthew 17:23. What parallel do you see?

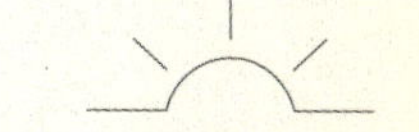

FOOD FOR THOUGHT

It is believed that the *land of Moriah* is the same area the Temple was built (2 Chronicles 3:1) and at its peak, the place where Jesus was crucified.

4. Abraham told the *young men* who accompanied them to stay *with the donkey* while he and Isaac went to *worship* God. Notice that although Abraham was told to sacrifice Isaac, he said, ***We** will come back to you* (Genesis 22:5). What does this suggest to you about what Abraham believed?

5. Read Genesis 22:6 and link it with John 19:17. What strikes you most about this scene?

6. As they walked *together*, Isaac asked his father a question. Use Genesis 22:7–8 to record and remark on:

   a. Isaac's question

   b. Abraham's response

      (1) Although Abraham spoke of his immediate situation, this was a prophetic word concerning the Lamb that God would ultimately *provide for Himself*. Use the following Scriptures to note and comment further on this provision:

      (a) John 1:29

      (b) 1 Peter 1:18–19

7. What do you find most notable about this divine test?

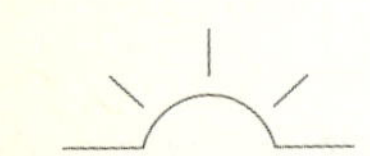

FOOD FOR THOUGHT

God never intended for Abraham to offer Isaac. Abraham was a prophet, and prophets not only spoke prophetically, sometimes they lived prophetically, and sometimes they acted things out prophetically. That's exactly what happened here: Abraham acted out the part of God the Father, and Isaac represented the Son, Jesus Christ.
—Pastor Brian Brodersen

THIRD DAY: Read Genesis 22:9–14

1. When they *came to the place* God indicated, Abraham prepared for the sacrifice. Use Genesis 22:9–10 to capture the intensity of this moment.

   a. Read Hebrews 11:17–19a to understand and comment on Abraham's perspective.

      (1) What does this indicate about Abraham's faith?

   b. Isaac was a young man: strong enough to carry the wood, strong enough to have resisted had he chosen to, and also old enough to understand the principle of sacrifice. With this in mind, what does his willingness to be laid *on the altar* suggest to you?

      (1) Link this with John 10:17–18 and share your thoughts.

2. As Abraham *took the knife to slay his son*, the Lord *called to him from heaven* (Genesis 22:11). From Genesis 22:12–14 cite and comment on:

   a. God's word to Abraham (verse 12)

FOOD FOR THOUGHT

Abraham trusted God, even when he did not feel like it. There is not a line in this text about how Abraham felt, not because he didn't feel, but because he walked by faith, not feelings.[24]
—Pastor David Guzik

(1) Pastor J. Vernon McGee says, *God spared Abraham's son, but God did not spare His own Son but gave Him up freely for us all.*[25] Connect this with Romans 8:32 and share what this means to you personally.

b. God's provision for Abraham (verse 13a)

c. Abraham's response (verses 13b–14)

(1) This was the first time in Scripture the name *Jehovah Jireh* (*The-LORD-Will-Provide*) was used. Considering the context, remark on the significance of this name of God.

(2) Share an area of your life in which you have experienced God as *Jehovah Jireh*.

3. Pastor David Guzik says, *Abraham didn't name the place in reference to what he experienced. He didn't name it Mount Trial or Mount Agony or Mount Obedience. Instead, he named the hill in reference to what God did; he named it Mount Provision. He named it knowing God would provide the ultimate sacrifice for salvation on that hill someday.*[26] What does this convey to you about the testing of your faith?

FOURTH DAY: Read Genesis 22:15–24

1. After Abraham had offered the ram on the altar, the Lord *called to Abraham a second time.* Once again, He acknowledged that Abraham had not *withheld* his *only son* (Genesis 22:15–16). Why do you think the Lord pointed this out a second time?

    a. By whom did God swear? See also Hebrews 6:13, 17–18.

        (1) Why is this significant?

2. Use God's *blessing* on Abraham in Genesis 22:17–18 to record and remark on:

    a. The number of Abraham's *descendants* (verse 17a)

    b. The strength of Abraham's *descendants* (verse 17b)

    c. The extent of the blessing on Abraham's *descendants* (verse 18a)

        (1) Why would God do all of this for Abraham? (verse 18b)

(a) How does this speak to you about the reward of obedience?

3. The promises of God to Abraham would continue through Isaac's descendants. This would require Isaac to have a wife of promise. Genesis 22:19–24 showed how God was already at work preparing Isaac's bride—Rebekah. What does this convey to you about God's promises?

4. What does your study today indicate to you about the way God views:

   a. Faith

   b. Obedience

FIFTH DAY: Read Genesis 23

1. Genesis 23 records the death and burial of Sarah. Her prominence is seen by the fact that she is the only woman to have the length of her life documented (Genesis 23:1). According to Genesis 23:2, how did Abraham react to Sarah's death?

a. What does this convey to you about their relationship?

2. After Sarah's death, Abraham *spoke to the sons of Heth*. What did he acknowledge about himself? Genesis 23:4a

   a. Considering the fact that God had promised Abraham this land, why was his statement remarkable?

   b. Link this with Hebrews 11:13–16 and share your thoughts.

3. What did Abraham request from the sons of Heth? Genesis 23:4b

   a. What does their response indicate about Abraham's witness among them? Genesis 23:5–6

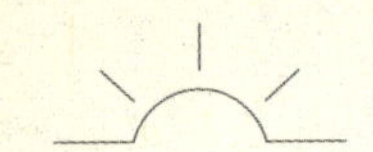

FOOD FOR THOUGHT

In the ancient world, land was linked to one's forefathers and held in trust for one's family. If Abraham had been gifted the land, it could have been reclaimed by the owner's family. However, because Abraham bought the land, he now had a legal deed and possessed a portion of the Promised Land. His ownership would last in perpetuity.

4. Negotiations then began for the purchase of a plot of land. From Genesis 23:9–18, note and comment on Abraham's demeanor during this process.

5. According to Genesis 23:19–20, Abraham buried Sarah in the *cave* of Machpelah. Read Hebrews 11:11 and 1 Peter 3:5–6 and record the synopsis of Sarah's life found in Scripture.

   a. What does this convey to you about the way God sees us?

SIXTH DAY: Review

1. Just as the promised birth of Isaac paralleled the birth of Jesus Christ, so too the offering of Isaac foreshadowed the sacrifice of Jesus on the cross. Fill in the chart to appreciate this comparison:

	ISAAC	JESUS	YOUR TAKEAWAY
The father's love	Genesis 22:2a	John 10:17	
The third day	Genesis 22:4	1 Corinthians 15:3–4	
The wood carried	Genesis 22:6a	John 19:17	
The provision for sacrifice	Genesis 22:8, 13–14	John 1:29	
The willingness to be offered	Genesis 22:9b–10	John 10:18	

a. With this remarkable comparison in mind, read John 8:56 and Galatians 3:8. How do you see the gospel being *preached beforehand* to Abraham?

(1) What do you find most amazing about this?

2. How has your study this week showcased the importance of faith in Our Great Creator?

NOTES

The Bride
GENESIS 24

FIRST DAY: Introduction

God has good plans for our lives! He works in a myriad of ways to fulfill His good plans. God is not only in the plans, but in the process:

- He leads us
- He guides us
- He accompanies us
- He assures us
- He prospers His work through us

What is needed, on our part, to experience the fulfillment of God's promises? Trust, cooperation, commitment, and prayer will make us full participants in the fulfillment of God's great plans.

This great truth is clearly portrayed in Genesis 24. God had promised Abraham that through his son, Isaac, a great nation would descend. Yet, Isaac was forty years old, without a prospect for a wife. Abraham commissioned his servant to travel 500 miles to a city in Mesopotamia. There Abraham's servant prayed for God to show him the right wife for Isaac. God immediately answered the servant's prayer. What followed was a process of negotiations, testimony, entrustment, and commitment. God was sovereignly working in all of the processes to fulfill and prosper His promises to Abraham.

Today God is working in the activity of your life to fulfill His promises to you!

Ask God to help you to cooperate with His process in fulfilling His promises to you.

SECOND DAY: Read Genesis 24:1–9

1. At this time, Abraham was 140 years old. Sarah had been buried, and his son, Isaac, was not yet married. What was written about Abraham in Genesis 24:1?

2. Abraham summoned his *oldest servant* to make a solemn oath by putting his *hand* under Abraham's *thigh* (Genesis 24:2). Use their conversation in Genesis 24:3–6 to remark on:

   a. The God he swore by (verse 3a)

   b. What the servant was *not* to do (verse 3b)

      (1) Link this with Deuteronomy 7:1, 3–4 and share your thoughts.

   c. What the servant was to do (verse 4)

   d. The servant's concern (verse 5)

   e. Abraham's warning (verse 6)

3. In Genesis 24:7–9 Abraham explained why Isaac should not leave Canaan with his servant. Use Abraham's statement to note and comment on:

   a. God's hand on Abraham (verse 7a)

   b. God's promise to Abraham (verse 7b)

      (1) How does this explain why he would not want Isaac to leave *this land*?

   c. Abraham's confidence (verse 7c)

      (1) Why do you think Abraham was so confident that God would do this?

   d. Abraham's charge (verses 8–9)

4. From your study today, how does Abraham's charge to his servant reveal:

   a. Abraham's wisdom

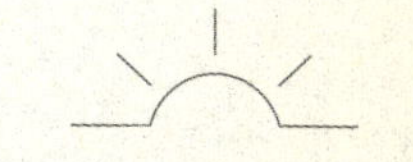

FOOD FOR THOUGHT

The Canaanites descended from the grandson of Noah (Genesis 9:24–25). They worshiped many gods: Ba'al Hadad, the god of the storm; Dagon, the god of fertility; as well as Ashtoreth and Anat, who were goddesses of sex and war.

b. Abraham's faith

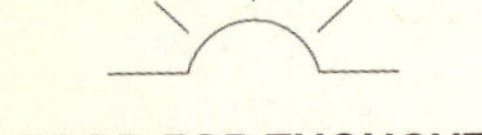

FOOD FOR THOUGHT

Note that Isaac, the son of promise, never left the Promised Land.

5. Share a way Abraham is an example to you.

THIRD DAY: Read Genesis 24:10–27

1. Abraham's *servant* left on his journey to find a bride for Isaac. Use Genesis 24:10–21 to describe:

   a. The journey (verses 10–11)

   b. The prayer (verses 12–14)

      (1) A thirsty camel could drink up to thirty gallons of water in fifteen minutes. Watering ten camels could require up to 300 gallons of water and at least an hour of hard labor. What does this convey to you about:

      (a) The servant's prayer

      (b) The kind of woman he sought for Isaac

c. The answer (verses 15–16)

(1) Why is it noteworthy that this happened *before he had finished speaking*?

(a) Link this with Isaiah 65:24. What do you see?

(b) How does this minister to you concerning prayer?

d. The confirmation (verses 17–21)

(1) What do you find most remarkable about this scene?

2. What did the servant do *when the camels had finished drinking*? Genesis 24:22

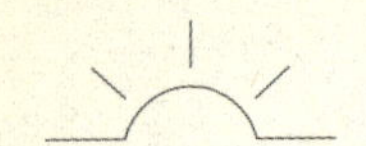

FOOD FOR THOUGHT

I think this is one of the most important verses in Scripture for those who are desiring to know how to be led of God.[27]
—Pastor Chuck Smith on Genesis 24:27

3. Rebekah told Abraham's servant she was from the family of Nahor and then responded to his request for lodging (Genesis 24:23–25). What do you find captivating about his response in Genesis 24:26–27?

   a. In what way(s) do you see the Lord leading this servant?

      (1) How does this speak to you?

4. Share a testimony of the Lord's leading in your life.

FOURTH DAY: Read Genesis 24:28–58

1. When Rebekah *ran and told her mother's household* about Abraham's servant, her brother Laban then *ran out* to meet him (Genesis 24:28–29). Use Genesis 24:30–33 to briefly summarize their encounter.

2. In Genesis 24:34 the *servant* introduced himself. He then declared the purpose of his *errand*. Read his account in Genesis 24:35–48 and record any observations that stand out to you.

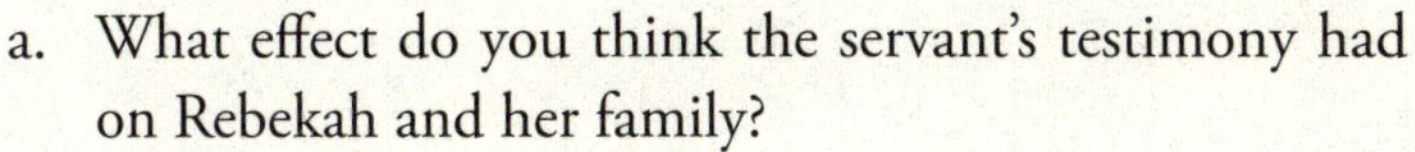

   a. What effect do you think the servant's testimony had on Rebekah and her family?

3. After relating his story, the servant asked Rebekah's family, *So tell me—will you or won't you show unfailing love and faithfulness to my master? Please tell me yes or no, and then I'll know what to do next* (Genesis 24:49 NLT). Why do you think he did this?

   a. Use Genesis 24:50–51 to remark on Bethuel and Laban's response.

4. According to Genesis 24:52–53, once the servant heard their response, what did he:

   a. Do (verse 52)

      (1) Notice this was the second time the servant did this. What does this convey about him?

   b. Give (verse 53)

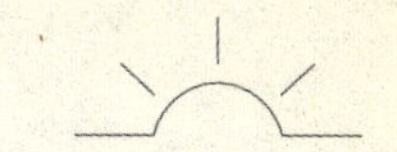

FOOD FOR THOUGHT

This is the longest recorded speech by any servant in the Bible—238 words.

(1) Observe that it was only after Rebekah's family responded positively to the servant's proposition that he blessed them with these gifts. Since it was part of the culture to give gifts to the family, this was considered a dowry—a promise of future security for the bride. Link this with Acts 2:38–39 and Ephesians 1:13–14 and share your thoughts.

5. After Abraham's servant had *stayed all night* with Rebekah's family, they tried to convince him to stay there *at least ten* more days (Genesis 24:54–55). However, what did the servant say? Genesis 24:56

6. When the servant insisted on leaving, Rebekah's family asked her if she would *go with* him (Genesis 24:57–58a). Print her response from Genesis 24:58b.

   a. How does this demonstrate Rebekah's faith?

      (1) Cite any parallels you observe between Rebekah's response and that of Abraham in Genesis 12:1–4.

(a) How does this confirm she was the right choice for the son of promise?

b. How do you desire to respond to God's call? See also Mark 10:29–30.

FIFTH DAY: Read Genesis 24:59–67

1. Once Rebekah decided to go with the servant to marry Isaac, her family willingly *sent* her (Genesis 24:59). Link the blessing they gave her in Genesis 24:60 with God's promise to Abraham in Genesis 22:17 and share your thoughts.

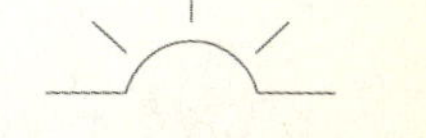

FOOD FOR THOUGHT

Beer Lahai Roi was the same well where Hagar encountered God. It means *The Well of the Living One Who Sees Me.* What an apt place for someone waiting for a wife!

2. After this, *the servant took Rebekah and departed.* Meanwhile, *Isaac came from the way Beer Lahai Roi* (Genesis 24:61–62). Use Genesis 24:63–65 to capture the moment Isaac and Rebekah met, making special note of:

   a. What Isaac was doing when he saw her (verse 63)

      (1) What does this suggest to you about the kind of man Isaac was?

   b. Rebekah's response (verses 64–65)

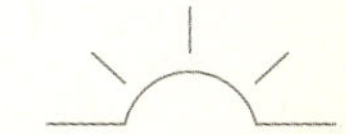

FOOD FOR THOUGHT

The veil was considered a sign of being betrothed. Rebekah's gesture showed that she had accepted the proposal.

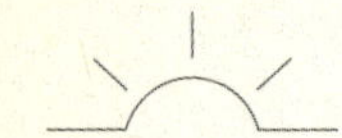

FOOD FOR THOUGHT

Sarah's tent would become Rebekah's home. This marked her as the matriarch and the most powerful woman in Abraham's tribe.

3. What happened after the *servant told Isaac all the things he had done*? Genesis 24:66–67

   a. Pastor Warren Wiersbe says, *The entire story makes it clear that God had chosen Rebekah for Isaac, for His providential leading is seen each step of the way.*[28] How does this underscore the importance of God's leading in relationships?

4. We have already seen how Isaac is in many ways a picture of Jesus. Use the chart below to understand and comment on the parallels between the story of Isaac and Rebekah and the relationship of Jesus and His Church:

ASPECT OF THE RELATIONSHIP	ISAAC AND REBEKAH	JESUS AND THE CHURCH	YOUR THOUGHTS
Faith	Genesis 24:58	1 Peter 1:8	
Union	Genesis 24:63–67a	Revelation 19:7–8	
Love	Genesis 24:67b	Ephesians 5:25–27	

SIXTH DAY: Review

1. Genesis 24 is rich in New Testament parallels. We see similarities between the relationship of Isaac and Rebekah and the relationship of Jesus and the Church. We also see in Abraham's servant a picture of the Holy Spirit's work and ministry. Use John 16:7–15 to cite any parallels you see between the ministry of Abraham's servant and that of God's Spirit.

2. From your study this week, share a brief impression of:
   a. Abraham

   b. The servant

   c. God's faithfulness

   d. Rebekah

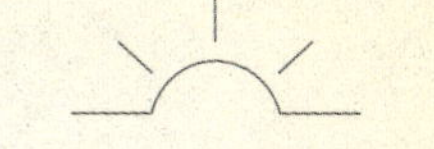

FOOD FOR THOUGHT

The servant refers to Abraham as his master twenty times in Genesis 24.

e. Laban

f. Rebekah's family

g. Isaac

3. What blesses you most about the plans and promises of Our Great Creator?

NOTES

NOTES

Isaac
GENESIS 25–26

FIRST DAY: Introduction

Being a recipient of the promises of God does not exempt you from deficits, conflicts, failures, and problems. Rather, it causes you to seek God in every deficit, conflict, failure, and problem for His direction. Life on earth is rife with difficulties. However, God will use those difficulties to move us to seek His Word, ways, and will.

Isaac was the promised son given by God to Abraham. He was also the heir to all the divine promises God gave to Abraham. However, Isaac's wife was barren until God answered his prayer. Rebekah's pregnancy was difficult, driving her to seek God. Isaac was forced to move his entire household more than once because of strife with the Philistines. God used even these difficulties in Isaac and Rebekah's lives to prompt them to pray and settle in the place where He could bless them.

As a believer, you are not exempt from deficits, conflicts, failures, and problems. However, God wants to use these difficulties to take you deeper into His promises and blessings.

Take a moment to entrust any present deficits, conflicts,
failures, or problems to God.

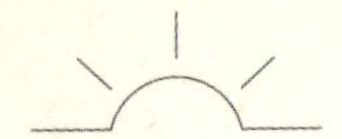

FOOD FOR THOUGHT

Keturah is mentioned in 1 Chronicles 1:32 as Abraham's concubine. In those days, a concubine was considered a secondary wife. She would not have held the same prominence as Sarah.

SECOND DAY: Read Genesis 25:1–18

1. The beginning of Genesis 25 summarizes the last days of Abraham's life. After the death of Sarah, Abraham married Keturah, who *bore him* many children (Genesis 25:1–4). What do you find interesting about this?

2. According to Genesis 25:5, what did Abraham give Isaac?

   a. Remembering that Isaac was the son of promise (like Jesus), link this with John 3:35. What do you see?

3. Abraham also *gave gifts* to the sons of his *concubines*. What did he do next? Genesis 25:6

   a. Why do you think he deemed this necessary?

4. Genesis 25:7–10 records the death of Abraham. Use these verses to note and comment on:

   a. Abraham's life

      (1) Link this with Psalm 92:12–15 and share your thoughts.

b. Abraham's burial

5. God *blessed* Isaac after the death of his father (Genesis 25:11). What does this indicate concerning God's promises to Abraham?

6. Genesis 25:12–18 documents the *genealogy of Ishmael.* Link this record with God's promise to Abraham in Genesis 17:20. What do you see?

7. What stands out to you about the life and legacy of Abraham?

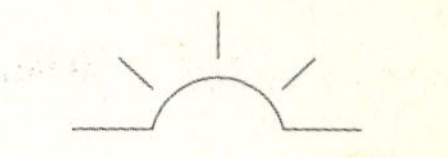

FOOD FOR THOUGHT

Abraham's death is recorded before the birth of Esau and Jacob. However, Abraham lived until they were fifteen years old.

THIRD DAY: Read Genesis 25:19–34

1. Following the *genealogy* of Ishmael, the text returned to the life of Isaac and his wife, Rebekah (Genesis 25:19–20). According to Genesis 25:21a, why did Isaac plead with the Lord *for his wife*?

   a. How did God respond? Genesis 25:21b

(1) Based on Genesis 25:26, we know that Isaac and Rebekah were married twenty years before the Lord answered. What does this suggest to you concerning prayer? See also Luke 18:1 and 1 John 5:14–15.

2. From Genesis 25:22a describe Rebekah's pregnancy.

   a. What did she do in response to this? Genesis 25:22b

      (1) Observe that both Isaac and Rebekah went to the Lord with their problems. How does this speak to you?

3. Record and remark on the Lord's response to Rebekah's inquiry. Genesis 25:23

4. Rebekah gave birth to twin sons as God had said (Genesis 25:24). Use Genesis 25:25–28 to contrast the two boys in the following chart:

	ESAU	JACOB	YOUR THOUGHTS
Birth	Verse 25	Verse 26	
Lifestyle	Verse 27a	Verse 27b	
Parental Preference	Verse 28a	Verse 28b	

a. Having observed the lives of Jacob and Esau, why do you think it was necessary for Rebekah to receive a personal word from God?

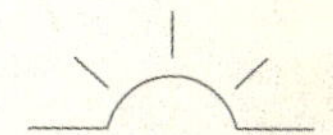

FOOD FOR THOUGHT

The Hebrew word *tam (mild)* used to describe Jacob actually implies being wholesome or upright.

5. Genesis 25:29–34 records an important interaction between Esau and Jacob. Use these verses to note and comment on:

   a. Esau's desire (verses 29–30)

   b. Jacob's bargain (verses 31, 33–34)

   c. Esau's reasoning (verse 32)

(1) The birthright included the spiritual promises given to Abraham by God as well as a double portion of the inheritance, the headship of the family, and the spiritual leadership. With this in mind, what does the fact that Esau *despised his birthright* indicate about him? See also Hebrews 12:16.

(2) Jacob's name means *heel-catcher* or *supplanter*. How does this incident show he was rightly named?

(3) Recall that God had told Rebekah in Genesis 25:23 that *the older shall serve the younger*. That being the case, why were Jacob's actions unnecessary?

6. From your study today, share a lesson or caution you receive from the actions and/or attitudes of:

   a. Isaac

   b. Rebekah

   c. Esau

   d. Jacob

FOURTH DAY: Read Genesis 26:1–14

1. According to Genesis 26:1, there was a *famine in the land* that caused Isaac to go to Abimelech in Gerar. At this time, *the LORD appeared to him*. Use God's word to Isaac in Genesis 26:2–5 to note and comment on:

    a. God's prohibition (verse 2a)

    b. God's directive (verses 2b–3a)

    c. God's promise (verses 3b–4)

    d. God's affirmation of Abraham (verse 5)

2. Isaac obeyed God's word and *dwelt in Gerar* (Genesis 26:6). From Genesis 26:7–11 summarize what happened while he and Rebekah were living there.

    a. Scan Genesis 12:10–20 and 20:1–18 and note your observations.

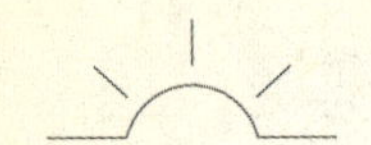

FOOD FOR THOUGHT

Abimelech was a title (not a name) used for the kings of the Philistines.

(1) Link this with Psalm 105:13–15 and share your thoughts.

3. From Genesis 26:12–14 describe God's blessing upon Isaac.

   a. How does this fulfill God's promise to Isaac in Genesis 26:3a?

      (1) How does this minister to you?

FIFTH DAY: Read Genesis 26:15–35

1. The Philistines *envied* Isaac's prosperity (Genesis 26:14b). As a result, what did they do? Genesis 26:15

   a. In addition, what did Abimelech tell Isaac to do? Genesis 26:16

(1) Observe that this conflict took place as God was blessing Isaac. What do you find noteworthy about this?

2. Use Genesis 26:17–22 to record Isaac's journey:

LOCATION	WHAT HAPPENED THERE	YOUR TAKEAWAY
The Well of Esek *Contention*	Verses 16–20	
The Well of Sitnah *Hostility*	Verse 21	
The Well of Rehoboth *Broad, Spacious Places*	Verse 22	
Shebah *Beersheba* *Well of Seven*	Verses 23–25	

a. Notice that Isaac continued to move on when conflict arose. Link his response with the following verses and share your thoughts:

(1) Psalm 34:14

(2) Romans 12:18

3. When Isaac settled in Beersheba, Abimelech paid him a visit. What do you observe about the interaction between Abimelech and Isaac? Genesis 26:26–31

a. What does Abimelech's assessment of Isaac convey to you about the son of promise?

4. What happened the *same day* that Abimelech came? Genesis 26:32–33

a. How do you think the events of that *same day* validated God's promise to Isaac?

5. Remark on the footnote in Genesis 26:34–35 concerning Esau.

a. What does this suggest about Esau's attitude concerning his family lineage? See Genesis 24:3.

6. What is your greatest takeaway from today's lesson?

SIXTH DAY: Review

1. From your study this week, record a lesson about the following:

    a. Barrenness

    b. Discomfort

    c. Disunity

    d. Difficulty

    e. Fear

    f. Conflict

    g. Direction

    h. Blessing

2. What did you observe in your lesson this week concerning Our Great Creator?

NOTES

Jacob's Deception
GENESIS 27–28

FIRST DAY: Introduction

God's grace is extensive and wonderful! Even when we take matters into our own hands and preempt His perfect timing, creating strife, God is ready to forgive (Psalm 86:5) and reinstate us in His promises. That is wonderful grace!

God promised He would bless Jacob instead of Esau (Genesis 25:23). However, when Rebekah overheard Isaac planning to do the contrary, she took matters into her own hands. She drew Jacob into a conspiracy to deceive Isaac and procure the ancestral blessing. Though they successfully obtained the blessing, the deception brought enmity between the brothers, which forced Jacob to leave his parents and seek refuge 500 miles away with his mother's brother.

Alone and exiled on his way to Padan Aram, God met Jacob with a heavenly revelation and His blessing. By this, God indicated His intention to still bless Jacob and fulfill the word He promised.

Have you taken matters into your own hands? Have you felt the disastrous effects of your own schemes? Take heart, God is ready to forgive! Isaiah 30:18 states that, *The Lord will wait, that He may be gracious to you.* He waits until our ways fail, and we are alone and forsaken, not knowing what our future holds. He then forgives us and reinstates us in His promises.

Ask God to reveal to you the wonder of His great grace!

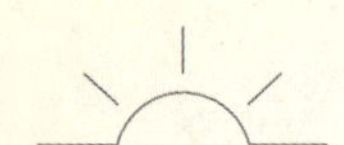

FOOD FOR THOUGHT

Before a father died, he would a perform a ceremony of blessing, in which he would officially hand over the birthright to the rightful heir. Although the firstborn son was entitled to the birthright, it was not actually his until the blessing was pronounced. The father could take the birthright away from the oldest son and give it to a more deserving son. However, after the blessing was pronounced, the birthright could no longer be removed. This is why fathers usually waited until the sons were grown so they could know the character of the sons before giving the blessing. Although Esau had sold his birthright to his younger brother years before, Jacob still needed his father's blessing to make it official.

SECOND DAY: Read Genesis 27:1–29

1. Isaac had grown old, and feeling his death was imminent, he called Esau to himself (Genesis 27:1–2). Use Genesis 27:1–4 to note and comment on:

   a. Isaac's condition (verses 1–2)

   b. Isaac's desire (verses 3–4a)

   c. Isaac's purpose (verse 4b)

      (1) According to Genesis 25:23, God had said, *The older shall serve the younger.* Typically, the patriarchal blessing would have been given before the entire family (Genesis 49). Yet, Isaac requested to meet alone with Esau. What do these actions convey about Isaac?

2. According to Genesis 27:5, *Rebekah was listening when Isaac spoke to Esau.* After Esau left to *hunt game*, Rebekah concocted a scheme. Summarize this scheme from Genesis 27:6–10.

a. Recalling the promise of Genesis 25:23, why was Rebekah's scheme unnecessary?

3. From Genesis 27:11–12, identify and remark on Jacob's concern with his mother's scheme.

a. How did Rebekah respond to Jacob's concern? Genesis 27:13

4. Jacob obeyed his mother's instructions. Use Genesis 27:14–25 to describe and comment on:

a. The preparation (verses 14–17)

b. The deception (verses 18–25)

(1) What do you find most disturbing about this entire situation?

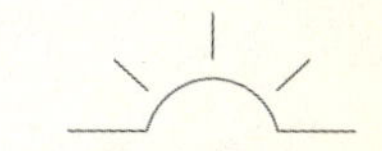

FOOD FOR THOUGHT

Jacob used five different elements of deceit: goat skins, cooked goat, his brother's clothes, alcohol, and lies.

5. After he had eaten, Isaac called his *son* over to embrace and bless him (Genesis 27:26–27a). Use Genesis 27:27b–29 to note:

   a. The goodness of the blessing (verse 27)

   b. The gift of the blessing (verse 28)

   c. The greatness of the blessing (verse 29)

6. From your study today, share a warning or caution you receive from the actions of:

   a. Isaac

   b. Rebekah

   c. Jacob

THIRD DAY: Read Genesis 27:30–46

1. After Isaac unwittingly blessed Jacob, Esau returned *from his hunting* (Genesis 27:30). Use the scene in Genesis 27:31–38 to highlight and remark on:

   a. Isaac's realization (verses 31–33, 35)

(1) Pastor Warren Wiersbe notes, *He knew that the Lord had overruled his own selfish plan so that his favorite son did not receive the blessing.*[29] How does this explain Isaac's reaction?

b. Esau's plea (verses 34, 36b, 38)

(1) Link this with Hebrews 12:16b–17 and share your thoughts.

c. Jacob's *deceit* (verses 35–36a)

d. Isaac's blessing (verses 33b, 37)

2. Genesis 27:39–40 (NLT) says: *Finally, his father, Isaac, said to him, "You will live away from the richness of the earth, and away from the dew of the heaven above. You will live by your sword, and you will serve your brother. But when you decide to break free, you will shake his yoke from your neck."* What stands out to you from Isaac's blessing for Esau?

3. Not surprisingly, *Esau hated Jacob* for what he had done. As a result, what did Esau plot to do? Genesis 27:41

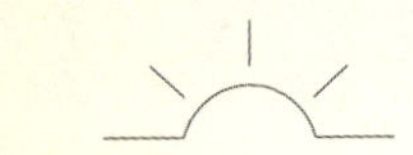

FOOD FOR THOUGHT

Although this was meant to be a short-term solution, Jacob would be gone for twenty years, and Rebekah would die without ever seeing her son again.

a. When Rebekah found out about this plot, what did she instruct Jacob to do? Genesis 27:42–45

4. From Genesis 27:46 record Rebekah's emotional state.

a. How does this explain her actions?

5. In response to your lesson today, what did you glean about the importance of waiting on the Lord? See also Psalm 37:34 and Isaiah 30:18.

FOURTH DAY: Read Genesis 28:1–9

1. After Rebekah expressed her concern that Jacob might marry a Canaanite woman, what did Isaac charge Jacob to do? Genesis 28:1–2

a. How is this reminiscent of Abraham's charge concerning Isaac? See Genesis 24:3.

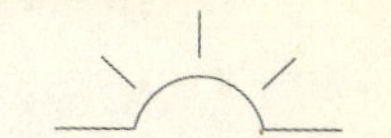

FOOD FOR THOUGHT

Esau married two Canaanite women, which further showed his disregard and disqualification for this spiritual blessing (Genesis 26:34–35 and 27:46).

2. Briefly highlight the blessing Isaac pronounced upon Jacob. Genesis 28:3–4

a. Recall that Isaac had tried to bless Esau against God's word. How does this blessing indicate Isaac's change of heart? See also Hebrews 11:20.

b. Why do you think Isaac emphasized *the blessing of Abraham*?

3. From Genesis 28:5 document Jacob's departure.

4. Esau observed all of these proceedings. Use Genesis 28:6–8 to record what Esau *saw*:

a. Verse 6

b. Verse 7

c. Verse 8

(1) Esau tried to requalify for the lost blessing by marrying a third wife who was a woman with ties to Abraham through Ishmael (Genesis 28:9). What does this action indicate to you about Esau?

5. What difference do you note between the way that Esau and Jacob:

   a. Felt about the blessing

   b. Sought to receive the blessing

      (1) Why do you desire God's blessing?

FIFTH DAY: Read Genesis 28:10–22

1. After being blessed and sent out by Isaac, Jacob journeyed *toward Haran*. Along the way, he stopped for the night and *found a stone and put it at his head* (Genesis 28:10–11). From Genesis 28:12 describe what he *dreamed* about as he slept.

a. This dream symbolized God's blessing. Link this with John 1:51. What do you see?

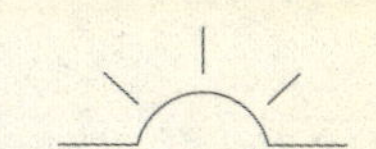

FOOD FOR THOUGHT

God's time to visit His people with His comfort is when they are most destitute of other comforts, and other comforters. [30]
—Matthew Henry

2. *The* Lord *stood above* the ladder in Jacob's dream and spoke to him for the first time. Notice how God identified Himself to Jacob in Genesis 28:13a. Why do you think this was significant?

3. Use the chart to note the continuity of God's blessing:

	LAND	DESCENDANTS	SEED
Abraham	Genesis 17:8	Genesis 17:6–7	Genesis 22:18
Jacob	Genesis 28:13b	Genesis 28:13c–14a	Genesis 28:14b

4. Print God's promise to Jacob. Genesis 28:15

a. Considering Jacob's circumstances, how do you think God's promise would have ministered to him?

b. In ancient times, it was commonly believed that if you left home, you left your gods behind. With this in mind, why was God's word to Jacob so revelatory?

c. Link this promise with the following Scriptures to note the necessity of God's presence:

(1) Exodus 33:14

(2) Deuteronomy 31:6

(3) Matthew 28:20b

(4) Hebrews 13:5b–6

(a) What assurance do you receive from this?

5. After this amazing dream, *Jacob awoke from his sleep*. From Genesis 28:16–22 note and comment on:

a. Jacob's reaction (verses 16–17)

b. Jacob's actions (verses 18–19)

(1) Note that the name *Bethel* means *house of God.* How does this enhance your understanding of Jacob's experience?

c. Jacob's *vow* (verses 20–22)

(1) Share a time or place in which you became aware of the presence of God.

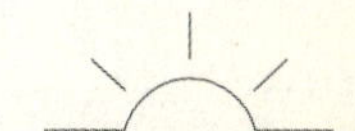

FOOD FOR THOUGHT

Jacob is the first and only patriarch to make a vow to God. Paying a tithe (a tenth) was an act of worship. The giver was acknowledging that everything he received was a gift from God.

6. From your study today, how do you see the grace of God manifested to Jacob?

a. How does this impact you?

SIXTH DAY: Review

1. From your study this week, share a way you can relate to the folly, failure, and forgiveness manifested through the lives of:

   a. Isaac

   b. Rebekah

   c. Jacob

2. Share something you received this week concerning the character of Our Great Creator.

NOTES

NOTES

Life with Jacob
GENESIS 29–30

FIRST DAY: Introduction

God graciously works in our lives to lead and direct us into all His good plans! In spite of our futile self-efforts, folly, and misguided notions, God faithfully works *all things together* for our good (Romans 8:28). In our lesson this week in Genesis 29 and 30, we witness God's overriding guidance and work in Jacob's life. Though Jacob misguidedly thought he was making things happen, he was in actuality being divinely guided, disciplined, protected, and blessed by God.

Isn't it good to know God's grace will prevail above our futile self-efforts, folly, and misguided notions to direct us into His good plans for our lives?

Ask God for a greater awareness of His gracious presence and direction in your life.

SECOND DAY: Read Genesis 29:1–14

1. After God's divine revelation to Jacob (Genesis 28:10–22), according to the Hebrew language, *he picked up his feet* (Genesis 29:1), meaning he was joyously propelled forward. What does this phrase convey to you about the effect of Jacob's encounter with God at Bethel?

2. As Jacob journeyed, he *came to the land of the people of the East* (Genesis 29:1b). Use Genesis 29:2–6 to answer the following:

   a. What did Jacob see when he arrived? (verse 2)

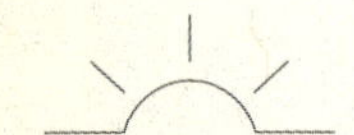

FOOD FOR THOUGHT

This type of well flows underground and bubbles up to the surface. By placing a stone over the mouth of the well, the weight of the stone would keep the water from coming up and evaporating on the open land. This type of well is also mentioned in Revelation 7:17.

   b. How were the *flocks* watered at this well? (verse 3)

   c. What did Jacob discover from the men at the well? (verses 4–6a)

   d. Who was *coming* at just that moment? (verse 6b)

3. Jacob observed, *Look, it's still broad daylight—too early to round up the animals. Why don't you water the sheep and goats so they can get back out to pasture?* (Genesis 29:7 NLT). How did the men respond? Genesis 29:8

   a. As Jacob *was still speaking* with them, Rachel arrived *with her father's sheep* (Genesis 29:9). What did Jacob do when he saw her? Genesis 29:10

      (1) What do you think motivated him to do this?

4. Knowing he had reached his destination and his mother's family, *then Jacob kissed Rachel, and lifted up his voice and wept.* After which he revealed who he was (Genesis 29:11–12a). Describe the response of Rachel and Laban from Genesis 29:12b–14.

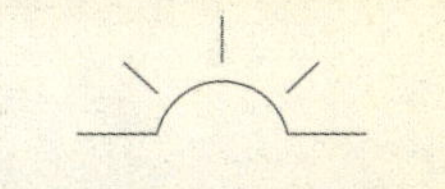

FOOD FOR THOUGHT

The first mention of a man kissing a woman in the Bible is found in Genesis 29:11.

5. From your study today, how do you see God directing Jacob's steps?

   a. Connect this with Proverbs 16:9 and Jeremiah 10:23. Share your insights.

THIRD DAY: Read Genesis 29:15–35

1. After Jacob stayed with his uncle for a month, what did Laban suggest? Genesis 29:15

2. What did Jacob offer in response? Genesis 29:18b

   a. Why did Jacob offer this? Genesis 29:18a

3. What do you learn about Laban's *two daughters* in Genesis 29:16–17?

4. Laban agreed to Jacob's terms (Genesis 29:19). From Genesis 29:20 remark on the *seven years* Jacob served Laban.

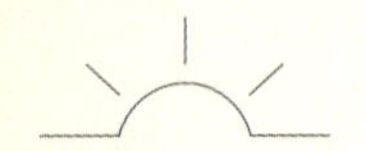

FOOD FOR THOUGHT

In that day, the custom was for the bride to be heavily veiled on her wedding day so that her face was not seen. This might explain why Jacob did not realize he had married Leah until the next morning.

5. After seven years, Jacob asked Laban for Rachel, and Laban held a wedding *feast* (Genesis 29:21–22). Use Genesis 29:23–30 to note and comment on:

   a. Laban's deception (verses 23–25)

      (1) Link this with the deception in Genesis 27:18–24. What ironies do you see?

   b. Laban's excuse (verse 26)

   c. Laban's proposition (verse 27)

d. Jacob's service (verses 28, 30b)

e. The consequences (verse 30a)

(1) Why do you think deception kept surfacing in Jacob's life?

(a) Consider this debacle in light of Galatians 6:7. What do you see?

6. *When the Lord saw that Leah was unloved*, He blessed her with children while *Rachel was barren* (Genesis 29:31). The names of each of Leah's sons held special significance for her. Use Genesis 29:32–35 to fill in the chart below concerning Leah's first four sons:

SON'S NAME	LEAH'S PERSPECTIVE	YOUR THOUGHTS
Reuben *See, a son*	Verse 32	
Simeon *One who hears*	Verse 33	
Levi *Attached*	Verse 34	
Judah *Praise*	Verse 35	

FOOD FOR THOUGHT

Most wedding celebrations lasted a week (seven days), so Leah's week-long wedding had to be finished before Jacob could marry Rachel.

a. What do the names of Leah's sons imply about:

(1) Her situation

(2) Her relationship with God (See also Isaiah 54:5)

7. The priestly tribe of Levi, the royal tribe of Judah, and the Messiah would descend from the unloved wife of Jacob. How does this minister to you?

FOURTH DAY: Read Genesis 30:1–21

1. Though Leah had all the disadvantages, God blessed her and made her fruitful. In contrast, use the following Scriptures to draw a portrait of Rachel:

a. Her advantages

(1) Genesis 29:9

(2) Genesis 29:17

(3) Genesis 29:20

b. Her demand (Genesis 30:1–2)

(1) What does Jacob's response reveal about Rachel's perceptions?

c. Her calculated solution (Genesis 30:3–4)

d. The names Rachel gave to her surrogate sons (Genesis 30:6–8)

(1) Dan (verse 6)

(2) Naphtali (verse 8)

e. Rachel's bargain (Genesis 30:14–15)

2. Leah was not only disadvantaged, but fell into competition with her sister. From Genesis 30:9–13, summarize Leah's reaction and response to Rachel's actions.

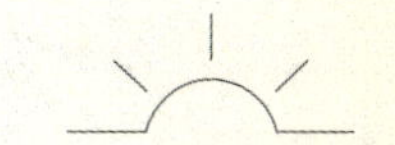

FOOD FOR THOUGHT

In the ancient world, mandrakes were a plant believed to have special fertility powers.

a. What do the names of Zilpah's sons convey to you about Leah's attitude:

(1) Gad (verse 11)

(2) Asher (verse 13)

3. Use Genesis 30:15–16 to describe the negotiations between the two sisters.

4. According to Genesis 30:17, *God listened to Leah* and allowed her to conceive again. Use the chart below to record and remark on the significance of the children God gave to Leah:

NAME	LEAH'S PERSPECTIVE	YOUR THOUGHTS
Issachar *Wages*	Genesis 30:18	
Zebulun *To dwell, honor*	Genesis 30:19–20	
Dinah *Justice*	Genesis 30:21—Jacob's only known daughter	

5. What differences do you observe between these two sisters?

FIFTH DAY: Read Genesis 30:22–43

1. In the Bible, whenever *God remembered* (or focused His attention on) someone, a blessing followed. What blessing followed when *God remembered Rachel*? Genesis 30:22

2. Why do you suppose it was important for Rachel to see that her conception had nothing to do with the mandrakes? Genesis 30:23

   a. How does God's mindfulness of Rachel minister to you?

3. From Genesis 30:24 note and comment on the name Rachel gave her son.

4. After *Rachel had borne Joseph*, Jacob asked Laban to release him and his family (Genesis 30:25–26). Why did Laban want Jacob to stay? Genesis 30:27

a. What do you find interesting about this?

5. Laban urged Jacob to stay and name his *wages* (Genesis 30:28). Use Genesis 30:29–33 to remark on:

   a. Jacob's service (verses 29–30)

   b. Jacob's request (verses 31–32)

   c. Jacob's integrity (verse 33)

6. Laban agreed to his request (Genesis 30:34). From Genesis 30:35–42 briefly summarize Jacob's self-efforts.

   a. Neither the Bible nor science give any credence to Jacob's method of manipulating the branches and bark. How would you characterize these self-efforts?

7. Jacob's acquired birthright and personal encounter with God guaranteed the divine blessing Laban observed on Jacob's life. Use Genesis 30:43 to note some of the specific ways God blessed Jacob.

    a. Take a moment to list a few specific ways God's blessing is evident in your life.

SIXTH DAY: Review

1. From your study this week, record a way that you see God's mercy and grace in the lives of:

    a. Jacob

    b. Leah

    c. Rachel

2. Share a way you have experienced the mercy and grace of Our Great Creator.

NOTES

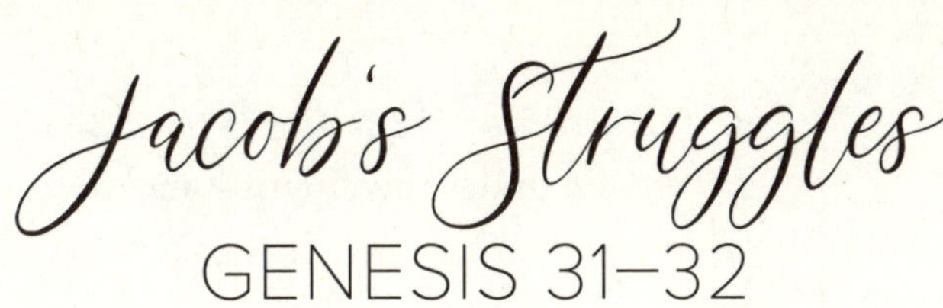

GENESIS 31–32

FIRST DAY: Introduction

Isn't it wonderful to consider that God never gives up on us! However, He will often use unrest, discomfort, and hard or unfair circumstances to propel us into His plans and build our faith. This is exactly what we see in Jacob's life.

Though Jacob's life was fraught with attempts to manipulate his circumstances to his own advantage, God was nevertheless with him. God protected, prospered, and progressively revealed Himself to Jacob. As Jacob labored twenty years in Laban's house, he began to realize God's presence with him and God's blessing upon him, even in the hardships he endured. God was bringing Jacob slowly to the end of his own nature that He might mold him into a man of faith.

God does not give up on His children! However, He often allows difficulties in our lives to work out our selfish nature and propel us to seek Him. God progressively reveals His presence with us, even in hard times, so that our faith might mature and grow.

Take a moment to thank God for His constant presence in your life.

SECOND DAY: Read Genesis 31:1–24

1. Even under the oppressive and oppositional conditions of Laban's employment, God's continued blessing on Jacob's life became obvious. As a result, according to Genesis 31:1–2, what did Jacob:

    a. Hear (verse 1)

    b. See (verse 2)

2. How do you see the circumstances in Jacob's life propelling him toward God's command? Genesis 31:3

   a. Why do you think God's promise to *be with* Jacob was crucial under the circumstances?

3. After receiving the Lord's command, Jacob *called Rachel and Leah to the field* to talk to them (Genesis 31:4). Use his words in Genesis 31:5–9 to contrast and comment on:

   a. Laban's maltreatment (verses 5a, 6–7a)

   b. God's favor (verses 5b, 7b–9)

4. Jacob told Rachel and Leah of a *dream* he had in which God indicated that He had directed the *flocks* to mate, and conceive to Jacob's advantage (Genesis 31:10–12a). Why did God do this? Genesis 31:12b

   a. Link this with Hebrews 4:13. How does this minister to you?

5. Record God's declaration to Jacob from Genesis 31:13.

   a. Recall Genesis 28:15–22 and share your observations.

6. In response to Jacob's announcement about leaving, Rachel and Leah said, *That's fine with us! We won't inherit any of our father's wealth anyway. He has reduced our rights to those of foreign women. And after he sold us, he wasted the money you paid him for us. All the wealth God has given you from our father legally belongs to us and our children. So go ahead and do whatever God has told you* (Genesis 31:14–16 NLT). What does this speech reveal about:

   a. Rachel and Leah

   b. Laban

7. From Genesis 31:17–21, briefly summarize Jacob's subsequent departure.

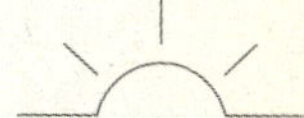

FOOD FOR THOUGHT

Perhaps *Rachel had stolen the household idols* as a good luck charm. These were the idols she had been raised to honor. According to some commentators, possession of these household idols indicated leadership in the family and were often used as divining tools, or a guarantee of inheritance, or property rights.

8. On the *third day* Laban discovered *that Jacob had fled*, so he *pursued* him (Genesis 31:22–23). Remark on what happened before Laban *overtook* Jacob. Genesis 31:24

9. From your study today, what evidence do you see of God's hand upon Jacob's life?

   a. Share a way this encourages you.

THIRD DAY: Read Genesis 31:25–55

1. After Jacob *stole away* and fled with all he had, *Laban overtook Jacob* in *the mountains* (Genesis 31:25). From Genesis 31:26–29, read Laban's rebuke of Jacob and comment on his claim.

   a. Had God not intervened, what do you think Laban intended to do to Jacob?

2. Laban accused Jacob of stealing his *gods* (Genesis 31:30). From Genesis 31:31–32, remark on Jacob's response.

3. Use Genesis 31:33–35 to describe Laban's search for his idols.

    a. What do you think of gods that can be stolen and hidden in such a fashion? See Isaiah 44:9–11.

4. Naturally, *Jacob was angry* with Laban because of this and *rebuked* him. Use Jacob's rebuke in Genesis 31:36–42 to note and comment on:

    a. Jacob's challenge to Laban (verses 36–37)

    b. Jacob's conduct toward Laban (verses 38–41)

    c. Laban's treatment of Jacob (verses 39b, 41b)

d. Jacob's testimony (verse 42)

(1) What does this account reveal to you about Jacob's progressive understanding of God?

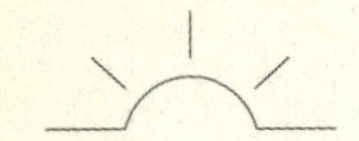

FOOD FOR THOUGHT

Jacob used the phrase, *the Fear of Isaac* in verses 42 and 53. This phrase can be translated, *the God that Isaac feared,* and implied that others should fear Him as well.

5. Incredibly, Laban still claimed ownership over *all* Jacob had, but acquiesced and made a *covenant* (Genesis 31:43–44). Use Genesis 31:45–55 to remark on the following about this *covenant*:

a. The monument (verses 45–48)

b. The invocation (verses 49–50)

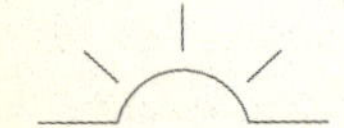

FOOD FOR THOUGHT

Mizpah was a word of suspicion and fear, not love and trust.

c. The agreement (verses 51–53)

(1) Notice that Laban swore by the *God of Abraham,* the pagan god of *Nahor*, and the god of *their father;* whereas, Jacob solely swore by the *Fear of Isaac*. What do you find interesting about this?

d. The sacrifice and parting (verses 54–55)

6. What stands out to you most about the confrontation between Laban and Jacob?

FOURTH DAY: Read Genesis 32:1–21

1. After Jacob went his way, *the angels of God met him* (Genesis 32:1). Why do you think it is noteworthy that this happened after Jacob parted from Laban?

   a. What did Jacob do when he *saw them*? Genesis 32:2

      (1) *Mahanaim* means *double camp*, signifying that the *camp* of God's angels was accompanying Jacob's *camp*. How do you think this revelation might have affected him?

      (2) This was the second time Jacob had seen the angels of God. Recall his first experience from Genesis 28:12. What do you think God was revealing to Jacob?

2. Jacob then *sent messengers to Esau* to announce his coming (Genesis 32:3). From Genesis 32:4–5 remark on the way Jacob addressed Esau in this message.

   a. What does this convey to you about Jacob?

3. The *messengers* reported back to Jacob that Esau was *coming to meet* him with *four hundred men* (Genesis 32:6). From Jacob's response in Genesis 32:7–8, record:

   a. How Jacob felt (verse 7a)

   b. What Jacob did (verse 7b)

   c. What Jacob reasoned (verse 8)

4. After his initial reaction, Jacob responded to the messengers' report by praying. Use his prayer in Genesis 32:9–12 to note and remark on:

   a. How Jacob addressed God (verse 9a)

   b. What God had *said* to Jacob (verses 9b, 12)

(1) Why do you think it helped Jacob to recall these promises?

(2) Recall a promise of God that ministered to you during a difficult circumstance.

c. What Jacob recognized or acknowledged (verse 10)

(1) How does this demonstrate a change in Jacob's attitude?

d. Jacob's plea (verse 11)

5. That night Jacob *lodged there* and prepared an exorbitant gift of over 550 livestock for Esau (Genesis 32:13–15). Use Genesis 32:16–20a to briefly summarize his instructions to *his servants* concerning this gift.

a. Observe Jacob's rationale for this in Genesis 32:20b. Considering that Jacob had just prayed and committed this situation to the Lord, what does this indicate?

6. After Jacob sent the *present* ahead, *he himself lodged that night in the camp* (Genesis 32:21). Why do you think Jacob did this?

   a. What does Proverbs 21:14 say about this?

7. From your lesson today, observe a way you see God pressing Jacob into greater faith.

   a. Share a way God has used hard circumstances to press you to greater faith.

FIFTH DAY: Read Genesis 32:22–32

1. After sending the *present* to Esau, Jacob took his family and servants *over the ford of Jabbok* ahead of him (Genesis 32:22–23). What happened when Jacob was *left alone*? Genesis 32:24

   a. What did the *Man* do *when He saw that He did not prevail* against Jacob? Genesis 32:25

2. In Jacob's weakened state, what did he refuse to do? Genesis 32:26

   a. Link this with Hosea 12:3–5 and record your insights about this struggle.

   b. Why do you think God *shrank* Jacob's hip muscle? See also 2 Corinthians 12:9–10.

3. The Man's response was to ask Jacob for his *name* (Genesis 32:27). A *name* in those days denoted the nature of a person. Why do you think it is significant that Jacob was given a new *name*? Genesis 32:28

   a. Bible scholars note that *Israel* means *God rules* or *God prevails*. Why was this a fitting new name for Jacob?

4. As a show of superiority, the *Man* would not reveal His *name* when Jacob asked; yet He still *blessed* Jacob (Genesis 32:29). Why is this noteworthy? See Hebrews 7:7.

5. Jacob called that place *Peniel*. What did Jacob recognize about the Man with whom he wrestled? Genesis 32:30

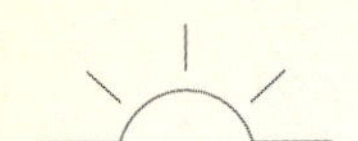

FOOD FOR THOUGHT

Note that *Peniel (Face of God)* is the location where Jacob met with God, but *Penuel* is a declaration about Jacob's new relationship with God.

a. According to John 1:18, why is this remarkable?

6. As the sun rose and Jacob *crossed over* to rejoin his family, *he limped on his hip* (Genesis 32:31). To commemorate this remarkable encounter, what do the Israelites do *to this day*? Genesis 32:32

7. Bible scholars have described the moment when Jacob wrestled with God, and God prevailed over Jacob, as the high point of his life. Why do you think this is so?

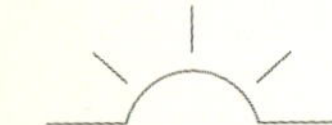

FOOD FOR THOUGHT

Warren Wiersbe said Jacob left this encounter with a new name, a new walk, and a new relationship with God.[31]

   a. From Jacob's testimony, what hope do you receive about your own losses or weaknesses?

SIXTH DAY: Review

1. From your study this week, share your greatest takeaway concerning Jacob's struggles with:
   a. Laban
   b. Esau
   c. God

2. Review the following Scriptures to note Our Great Creator's progressive revelation to Jacob:
   a. Genesis 31:3
   b. Genesis 31:5
   c. Genesis 31:7
   d. Genesis 31:9
   e. Genesis 31:11–12a
   f. Genesis 31:29
   g. Genesis 31:42
   h. Genesis 32:1–2a
   i. Genesis 32:9–10, 12
   j. Genesis 32:28–29

3. Share a way Our Great Creator has progressively revealed His presence to you.

NOTES

The Return
GENESIS 33–35

FIRST DAY: Introduction

Life is full of upheavals. One day might bring reconciliation and hope, while another produces tragedy, heartache, and turmoil. How can we maintain, let alone prosper, in such an unpredictable and fluctuating atmosphere? We can, by returning to the house of God and re-centering our lives around Him. Only God can lead us, secure us, and prosper us in such uncertain times.

This is the lesson Jacob learned. His life was rife with ups and downs. In the midst of his turmoil, God called him back to Bethel *(The House of God)*. There Jacob was reminded of his first encounter with God, His faithful care, and His promises.

In all our lives, there will be highs and lows, ups and downs, mountains and valleys. Since this is the condition of life, we need to continually re-center our lives upon the Lord and seek His direction.

Ask the Lord to help you to re-center your heart and thoughts on Him.

SECOND DAY: Read Genesis 33

1. Having wrestled all night with God, Jacob prepared to meet his brother. Use Genesis 33:1–14 to describe:

    a. What Jacob saw (verse 1a)

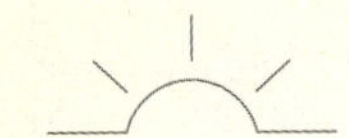

FOOD FOR THOUGHT

According to the Tel Amarna tablets, it is proper when greeting a king to bow to the earth seven times in approaching him.[32]
—Pastor Chuck Smith

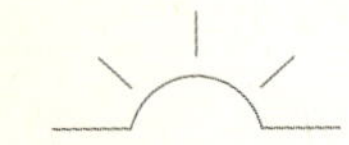

FOOD FOR THOUGHT

In Genesis 33:9 Esau told Jacob, *I have enough.* He used the Hebrew word *rab*, which means, *I have much.* In verse 11, Jacob used the same phrase, except he used the word *kol*, which means, *I have everything.*

b. What Jacob did (verses 1b–3)

c. Esau's response (verse 4)

d. The interaction between the brothers (verses 5–11)

(1) Use Genesis 27:41 to contrast this interaction with Esau's words from twenty years earlier. What do you find remarkable about this?

(2) What reason did Jacob give for his generosity to Esau? (verses 10–11)

(a) What does this demonstrate to you about Jacob?

e. Esau's suggestion to Jacob (verse 12)

f. Jacob's reply (verses 13–14)

2. Esau then suggested at least leaving some men with Jacob for protection, but Jacob said there was no *need* (Genesis 33:15). Use Genesis 33:16–18 to mark the brothers' departures and destinations on the map below:

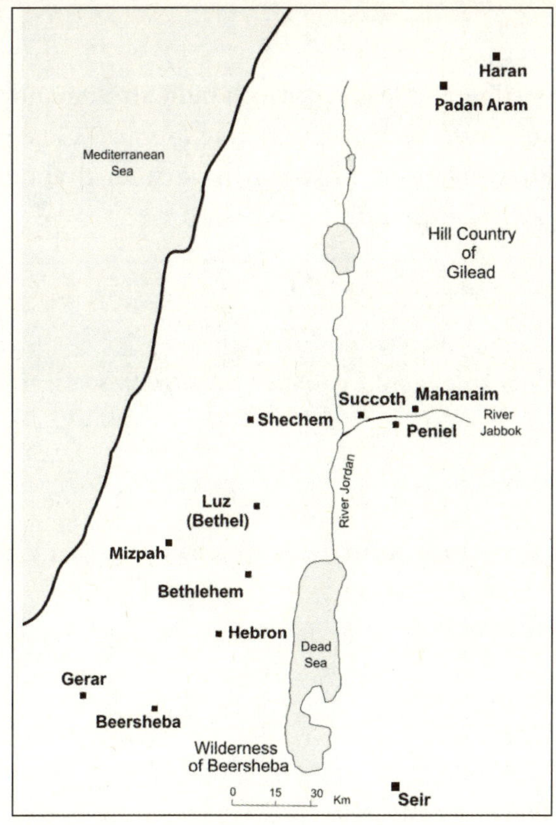

a. Where Esau settled (verse 16)

b. Where Jacob journeyed and settled (verses 17–18) *Also note Genesis 31:49; 32:2, 30.

(1) What did he do there?

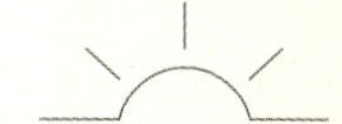

FOOD FOR THOUGHT

Succoth (Sukkot) means *booths* or *shelters. Succoth* is also a major Jewish festival *(The Feast of Booths/Tabernacles)*, which commemorates God's sheltering of the Israelites in the wilderness.

3. According to Genesis 33:18, *Jacob came safely to the city of Shechem.* Considering all of Jacob's encounters, why is this remarkable?

4. After settling in Shechem, Jacob built an altar and called it *El Elohe Israel,* or *The Mighty God of Israel* (Genesis 33:19–20). Drawing from what you have studied about Jacob, why is this a fitting title?

   a. What title would you give to your life's story?

5. Share something from the reconciliation of Jacob and Esau that ministers to you.

FOOD FOR THOUGHT

This occurrence serves to illustrate the low standard of morals prevalent among the Canaanites. Any unattended female could be raped. [33]
—H.C. Leupold

THIRD DAY: Read Genesis 34

1. While Jacob's family lived in Shechem, *Dinah the daughter of Leah* befriended the *daughters of the land* (Genesis 34:1). When she went to visit them, a man named Shechem *saw her*. Use Genesis 34:2–4 to answer the following questions:

   a. Who was Shechem? (verse 2a)

   b. What did he do? (verse 2b)

c. What did Shechem want? (verse 3)

d. What did he demand of *his father*? (verse 4)

2. This terrible incident provoked a variety of responses. From Genesis 34:5–12 share your thoughts about the responses of:

   a. Jacob (verse 5)

   b. Hamor (verses 6, 8–10)

      (1) Use Deuteronomy 7:3–4 to understand and comment on why it would be unwise for Jacob's family to follow Hamor's suggestion.

   c. The sons of Jacob (verse 7)

   d. Shechem (verses 11–12)

3. Use Genesis 34:13–19 to summarize:

   a. Jacob's sons' answer to Shechem (verses 13–17)

b. Shechem's response (verses 18–19)

4. After hearing the offer of the *sons of Jacob*, Hamor and Shechem went to persuade *the men of their city* to agree to it (Genesis 34:20). Use the words of Hamor and Shechem in Genesis 34:21–24 to note and comment on:

   a. Their persuasion (verse 21)

   b. The *condition* (verse 22)

   c. Their true motive (verse 23)

      (1) What stands out to you from the rationale of the men of Shechem?

   d. The response of *all who went out of the gate* (verse 24)

5. From Genesis 34:25–29 summarize what Dinah's brothers, Simeon and Levi, did when the men of Shechem *were in pain*.

6. The aftermath of Dinah's rape and her brothers' subsequent revenge created divergent perspectives in the family. Use Genesis 34:30–31 to contrast and remark on the perspective of:

   a. Jacob (verse 30)

   b. Simeon and Levi (verse 31)

7. Recall that God had commanded Jacob to return to the land of his family (Genesis 31:3, 13). Considering the debacle in Shechem, what warning or lesson do you receive?

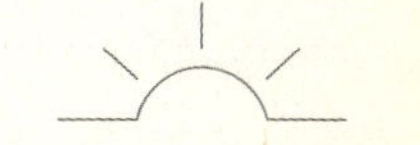

FOOD FOR THOUGHT

Note that God is not mentioned at all in Genesis 34. However, in Genesis 35, when Jacob returned to Bethel, God will be mentioned ten times.

FOURTH DAY: Read Genesis 35:1–15

1. Contrary to Jacob's dire prediction (Genesis 34:30), what hopeful directive did God give Jacob? Genesis 35:1

   a. Use Genesis 28:11–19 and 31:13a to underscore why Bethel was a good place for Jacob to *dwell*.

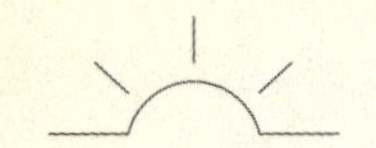

FOOD FOR THOUGHT

In the Bible, a change of garments symbolizes a new spiritual beginning, a change of character, or a change of position.

2. From Genesis 35:2, record Jacob's instructions to his family:

   a.

   b.

   c.

3. According to Genesis 35:3, what did Jacob intend to do at Bethel?

4. Use Genesis 35:4–8 to record your observations concerning:

   a. The family's cooperation (verse 4)

      (1) What does this pagan collection suggest to you about the spiritual condition of Jacob's family?

   b. God's protection (verses 5–6)

   c. Jacob's altar (verse 7)

   d. Rebekah's nurse (verse 8)

5. When Jacob reached Bethel, God *appeared* to him and *blessed* him (Genesis 35:9). What did God remind Jacob about:

   a. Jacob's name (verse 10)

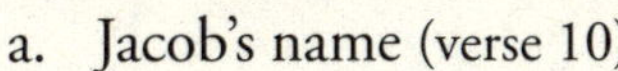

   b. God's name (verse 11a)

   c. The nation (verse 11b)

   d. The land (verse 12)

      (1) Why do you think this reminder was necessary?

      (2) Note that the blessing of God, which Jacob sought, was not fully his until he returned to Bethel. What does this suggest to you about God's promises?

6. How did Jacob honor the place God spoke to him? Genesis 35:13–15

7. From your study today, where do you need to be to receive the blessings and promises of God?

FOOD FOR THOUGHT

God revealed Himself to Jacob as *El Shaddai*. This is the same covenant name God revealed to Abram (Genesis 17:1).

FIFTH DAY: Read Genesis 35:16–29

1. Use Genesis 35:16–19 to summarize what happened as Jacob's family *journeyed* south from Bethel.

   a. Rachel's dying act was to name her son Ben-Oni, *son of my sorrow.* Why do you think Jacob changed his name to Benjamin, *son of my right hand*?

      (1) Interestingly, Rachel was not buried in the family crypt at Hebron (just fourteen miles away). From Genesis 35:19–20, describe Rachel's burial.

2. After *Israel journeyed and pitched his tent beyond the tower of Eder*, what folly did Reuben commit? Genesis 35:21–22

3. From Genesis 35:23–26, list Jacob's sons according to their mothers:

   a. Leah's sons

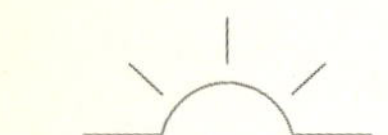

FOOD FOR THOUGHT

Reuben lost his birthright as the firstborn son because of his fornication with Bilhah. By the standards of that time, this could be interpreted as a challenge to usurp his father's leadership. Simeon and Levi forfeited their birthright because of their violence at Shechem, making Judah the son that received the promise of Abraham's Seed (the Messiah).

b. Rachel's sons

c. Bilhah's sons

d. Zilpah's sons

4. Use Genesis 35:27–29 to describe the last years of Isaac's life.

a. What do you find most interesting about this scene?

5. From your study this week, share a way you see God's faithful work in Jacob's life.

SIXTH DAY: Review

1. Write a brief impression of:

    a. Jacob

    b. Dinah

    c. Shechem

    d. Simeon and Levi

    e. Rachel

    f. Reuben

2. From your study this week, what have you observed about Our Great Creator?

NOTES

NOTES

Family Matters
GENESIS 36–38

FIRST DAY: Introduction

God does not choose perfect people for His service. Rather, God perfects those He chooses and qualifies them for His work.

Having disapproved Esau, God chose to entrust Jacob and his lineage with His promises, covenant, and blessings. However, the sons of Jacob were rife with problems. These future tribal leaders were dishonest, hateful, jealous, angry, untrustworthy, betrayers, arrogant, insensitive, deceitful, fearful, lascivious, and spiritually immoral. Yet God did not reject the clan of Jacob. Rather, He used these brothers' own vices to discipline them, lead them to repentance, and bring them into conformity with His will.

God's choosing and discipline of Jacob's sons is a cause for hope to all believers. God is not looking for perfection from us, but a willingness to confess our sin and allow Him to work His holy perfection in our lives. Philippians 2:13 reminds us that it is God who works in us both to will and to do for His good pleasure. God worked in the sons of Jacob, and He is working in our lives in order to bring us into the fullness of His promises, covenant, and blessings.

Ask God to perfect the work His has begun in you.

SECOND DAY: Read Genesis 36:1–43, 37:1–11

1. We will only be taking a cursory glance at the descendants of Esau listed in Genesis 36. However, what do you learn about the wives Esau chose for himself and his sons? Genesis 36:1–6

a. What does this convey to you about Esau?

2. Note and remark on the living arrangements of Jacob and Esau. Genesis 36:6–8

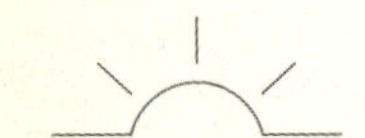

FOOD FOR THOUGHT

Although related to Jacob through Esau, the Edomites (Genesis 36:9) and Amalekites (Genesis 36:12) became long-standing enemies of Israel.

3. Genesis 36:1–43 documents the genealogy of Esau. Skim over this genealogy and record anything of note to you.

4. While Esau's descendants multiplied, became leaders, and made great land claims, Jacob *dwelt in the land where his father was a stranger* (Genesis 37:1–2a). Jacob's story then transitioned to the story of his sons. Remark on what happened when his son, Joseph, was *seventeen years old.* Genesis 37:2b

5. From Genesis 37:3–4 contrast and comment on the relationship between Joseph and:

a. His father (verse 3)

(1) The *tunic* Jacob made Joseph was a garment indicating privilege, status, and perhaps designating him as Jacob's successor. What problems do you see in Jacob's decision?

(2) Use Genesis 25:28 to compare this relationship with that of Jacob to Esau and their parents. What do you see?

b. His brothers (verse 4)

6. Joseph then *told* his family about two dreams he had (Genesis 37:5, 9), which exacerbated an already tense situation. Use Genesis 37:6–11 to fill in the chart concerning his dreams:

DREAM	DESCRIPTION	BROTHERS' REACTION	JACOB'S REACTION
Dream 1 *Verses 6–7*		Verse 8	
Dream 2 *Verse 9*		Verse 11a	Verses 10, 11b

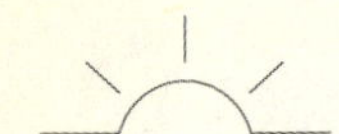

FOOD FOR THOUGHT

Dreams carried weight in ancient cultures as a form of divine communication, especially if the dream was given twice.

a. At this juncture, how would you characterize:

(1) Joseph

(2) Jacob

(3) Joseph's brothers

7. What do you find amazing about the fact that God chose to reveal His promises to Jacob's clan?

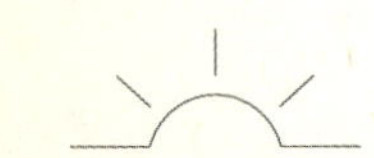

FOOD FOR THOUGHT

Dothan means *the place of two wells.* These two wells are still in existence today, one of which bears the name, *The Pit of Joseph.*

THIRD DAY: Read Genesis 37:12–36

1. One day when Joseph's *brothers* were out with *their father's flock in Shechem*, about fifty miles away, Jacob sent Joseph to check on them. *A certain man* directed Joseph to Dothan, fifteen miles further; there *he found them* (Genesis 37:12–17). What did Joseph's brothers conspire to do *when they saw him afar off*? Genesis 37:18

   a. What does this convey about the intensity of their feelings?

2. Use Genesis 37:19–20 to record and remark on their conspiracy.

   a. What does the word *conspired* suggest to you about the brothers?

3. Cite the alternative plan suggested by Reuben in Genesis 37:21–22a.

   a. Why did Reuben suggest this? Genesis 37:22b

4. Genesis 37:23–36 documents the violent treatment of Joseph by his brothers. Use these verses to describe and comment on:

   a. What they did to Joseph (verses 23–25a)

      (1) Remark on the fact that after doing this, *they sat down to eat a meal.*

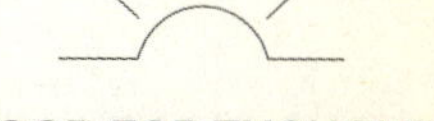

FOOD FOR THOUGHT

Reuben's attempt to save Joseph was not necessarily out of fraternal concern, but more likely an attempt to regain his status as the firstborn son of Jacob.

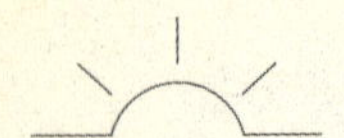

FOOD FOR THOUGHT

Early documents dating back to the 2nd millennium (2000–1000 BC) indicate that the average price for a slave was between 15–30 shekels. Ironically, Joseph was sold as a slave to the descendants of Abraham's slave, Hagar.

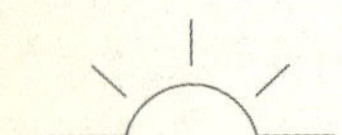

FOOD FOR THOUGHT

Jacob deceived his father Isaac with goatskins (Genesis 27:15–16); consequently, he was deceived by goat's blood.

b. Judah's suggestion (verses 25b–27)

c. The sale of Joseph (verse 28)

d. Reuben's failed rescue (verses 29–30)

e. The deception (verses 31–32)

f. Jacob's reaction (verses 33–35)

(1) Consider that Jacob's sons allowed their father to believe Joseph was dead for many years. What do you find most disconcerting about this?

g. Joseph's fate (verse 36)

5. Joseph is in many ways a type or picture of Jesus. Use the chart to note a few of these parallels:

	JOSEPH	JESUS	YOUR TAKEAWAY
Relationship with father	Genesis 37:3a	Luke 3:22	
Rule over brethren	Genesis 37:8a	Acts 2:36 Philippians 2:9–11	
Animosity of brothers	Genesis 37:4b, 8b	John 15:24b–25	
Sold	Genesis 37:28	Matthew 26:15	

FOURTH DAY: Read Genesis 38:1–11

1. Genesis 38 interrupted the story of Joseph to record an important event in the life of Judah. According to Genesis 38:1, what did Judah do *at that time*?

2. While he was with the Canaanites, Judah *saw a daughter of a certain Canaanite* and married her. They had three sons: Er, Onan, and Shelah (Genesis 38:2–5). According to Genesis 38:6, Judah *took* a woman named Tamar as *wife for Er his firstborn*. Use Genesis 38:7–10 to note and comment on the fate of Er and Onan.

a. Although Onan's obligation was part of ancient culture, the Law of Moses addressed it further. Use Deuteronomy 25:5–9 to understand and remark on Onan's wrongdoing.

b. It would appear that Judah's oldest sons were irredeemable. What does this suggest to you about God's plans?

3. As was customary, Judah told Tamar to *remain a widow* in her father's house until his youngest son, Shelah, was old enough to marry her (Genesis 38:11a). However, what did Judah intend? Genesis 38:11b

4. From what you have studied thus far, what is your opinion of Judah and his lineage?

5. Why is it remarkable to you that God would later establish the dynasty of Israel (the House of David) through Judah?

FIFTH DAY: Read Genesis 38:12–30

1. *In the process of time*, Judah's wife died. After he was *comforted*, he went with his friend Hirah to *shear his sheep*. When Tamar was informed of this, what did she do? Genesis 38:12–14a

   a. Why did she do this? Genesis 38:14b

   b. What happened *when Judah saw her*? Genesis 38:15–16a

      (1) Clearly Tamar knew she would be able to deceive Judah in this way. What does this suggest to you about Judah?

2. Use Genesis 38:16b–23 to summarize what happened between Judah and Tamar.

3. *Three months after*, Judah was told that Tamar was *with child by harlotry* (Genesis 38:24a). What do you think of his reaction to this news? Genesis 38:24b

4. Use Genesis 38:25 to capture the plot twist in this story.

5. What drastic change do you see in Judah's attitude and life? Genesis 38:26

   a. Link Judah's confession with 1 John 1:9 and share your thoughts.

6. Describe the birth of Tamar's *twins* from Genesis 38:27–30.

   a. As a son of Judah, Perez would become part of the Messianic line, an ancestor of Jesus Christ (Luke 3:33). Furthermore, Tamar was included in Jesus' genealogy in Matthew 1:3. What do you find most remarkable about this?

      (1) How does the inclusion of these people into the Messianic line minister to you?

7. Share a way you see the grace of God at work in the family of Jacob.

SIXTH DAY: Review

1. From your study this week, share your greatest takeaway about:

    a. Jacob

    b. Joseph

    c. Joseph's brothers

    d. Reuben

    e. Judah

    f. Tamar

2. From Genesis 36–38, what do you find most notable about the ways of Our Great Creator?

NOTES

Joseph's Testings
GENESIS 39–41

FIRST DAY: Introduction

From the time you start school, life is full of testings. Tests prove what you know, what you still need to learn, and your readiness to advance. Life is also filled with spiritual tests. Spiritual tests take many forms, but they all try our faith. In the end, they prove whether or not we trust God, His Word, and His promises.

In Genesis 39, 40, and 41, we witness the testing of Joseph. Before God promoted Joseph to the office of Prime Minister of Egypt, He tested him. Joseph was tested by:

- Slavery
- Responsibility of a great household
- Sexual temptation
- False accusations
- Slander
- Imprisonment
- Disappointment
- Delay

In all these tests, Joseph excelled by continually seeking to please God. God was with Joseph and blessed him through all his testings.

Let Joseph's life be an inspiration to you! God uses testings in our lives to prepare us for all He has in store for us. By faith, trusting in, and walking with God, we will not only survive, but excel in these tests.

Ask God to deepen your trust in Him, His Word,
and His promises to excel in life's testings.

SECOND DAY: Read Genesis 39

1. Following the situation between Judah and Tamar in Genesis 38, the story of Joseph resumed in Genesis 39. After he was sold into slavery, Joseph was *taken down to Egypt* and sold to Potiphar, Pharaoh's *captain of the guard* (Genesis 39:1). Use Genesis 39:2–6a to cite phrases that indicate:

    a. The Lord's presence and *blessing*

    b. Potiphar's *favor*

        (1) How does God's presence with Joseph while in captivity minister to you?

2. Genesis 39:6b notes that Joseph was a *handsome* man, which created an issue with *his master's wife.* Use Genesis 39:7–12 to comment on:

    a. The advances of Potiphar's wife (verses 7, 10a, 11–12a)

    b. The responses of Joseph (verses 8–9, 10b, 12b)

(1) According to Genesis 39:9c, how did Joseph characterize such an act? See also Psalm 51:4.

(a) Link Joseph's response to temptation with the following and share how it speaks to you:

(1) 1 Corinthians 6:18

(2) 2 Timothy 2:22

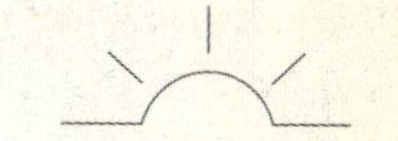

FOOD FOR THOUGHT

This is the second time Joseph was stripped of his cloak and had his garment used for a false report.

3. When Joseph rejected the advances of Potiphar's wife, what did she do? Genesis 39:13–18

a. As a result of her *words*, what did Potiphar do? Genesis 39:19–20

4. In spite of this injustice toward Joseph, describe and remark on God's *favor*. Genesis 39:21–23

5. Share a way you have experienced God's presence or favor in the midst of a trial.

6. From your study today, what impresses you most about Joseph?

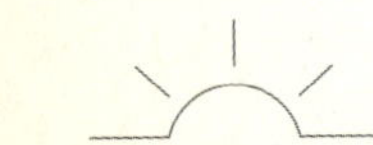

FOOD FOR THOUGHT

The *captain of the guard* was Potiphar himself (see Genesis 39:1). The fact that Potiphar put Joseph in prison instead of having him executed may suggest he did not believe his wife, and only cast Joseph into prison to save face.

THIRD DAY: Read Genesis 40

1. According to Genesis 40:1–3, what happened while Joseph was *in the prison*?

2. When the *captain of the guard* put the *butler* and *baker* in Joseph's care, Joseph served them (Genesis 40:4). The Hebrew word *served* can also mean *waited upon or ministered to.* Considering Joseph's own situation, why is it remarkable that he *served* these men?

3. What happened after the *butler* and *baker* had been *in custody for a while*? Genesis 40:5

   a. From Genesis 40:6–7, observe Joseph's attentiveness toward them. What does this convey to you about Joseph?

4. The *butler* and *baker* told Joseph that they each had a dream, but there was no *interpreter*. When Joseph offered to interpret their dreams, who did he reveal as the source of *interpretations*? Genesis 40:8

5. The *butler* and *baker* then proceeded to tell Joseph their dreams. Use Genesis 40:9–22 to fill in the chart concerning these dreams:

	DREAM	MEANING	FULFILLMENT
Butler	Verses 9–11	Verses 12–13	Verses 20–21
Baker	Verses 16–17	Verses 18–19	Verse 22

6. Joseph asked the *butler* to *make mention* of him to Pharaoh when he was restored (Genesis 40:14–15). However, what happened when the *butler* was released? Genesis 40:23

   a. Although Joseph trusted and honored God in his imprisonment, this must have been a disheartening and difficult trial. Read Psalm 105:17–19 to further understand and remark on what God was doing in Joseph during this time.

7. From your study today, share a way Joseph is an example to you.

FOURTH DAY: Read Genesis 41:1–32

1. *Two full years* passed after the butler was released from prison. Then one night, *Pharaoh had a dream* (Genesis 41:1a). Use Genesis 41:1b–7 to briefly describe the *dream* Pharaoh had about:

   a. The *seven cows* (verses 1b–4)

   b. The *seven heads of grain* (verses 5–7)

2. *In the morning,* Pharaoh was *troubled* by his dreams. What was his dilemma? Genesis 41:8

   a. It was at this moment that the *butler* remembered his *faults* in forgetting Joseph (Genesis 41:9). What did he tell Pharaoh? Genesis 41:10–13

3. At this news, *Pharaoh sent and called Joseph* from prison. Use Genesis 41:14 to capture the drama of Joseph's release from prison.

a. Now after thirteen years of testing, Joseph was brought out *quickly*. What does this convey to you?

4. Pharaoh told Joseph he *had a dream* and *heard* Joseph could *interpret it* (Genesis 41:15). What stands out to you from Joseph's response in Genesis 41:16?

5. Pharaoh recounted his dreams to Joseph (Genesis 41:17–24). Summarize the interpretation using Genesis 41:25–31.

   a. Why was it significant that *the dream was repeated*? Genesis 41:32

6. What is your greatest takeaway from today's study?

FIFTH DAY: Read Genesis 41:33–57

1. God had used Joseph to interpret Pharaoh's dreams and warn of their imminent fulfillment. Use Genesis 41:33–36 to highlight the advice Joseph gave in light of the impending *famine*.

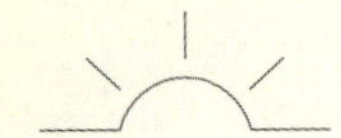

FOOD FOR THOUGHT

This is the first mention in the Bible of the Holy Spirit coming upon someone—and it was acknowledged by a pagan ruler!

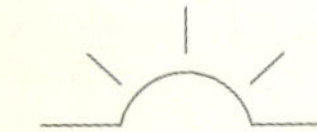

FOOD FOR THOUGHT

A signet ring was used to seal official documents and carried the owner's authority and approval.

a. Remark on the response of Pharaoh and his *servants* to Joseph's *advice*. Genesis 41:37–38

2. Use Genesis 41:39–45 and Psalm 105:20–22 to note and comment on the following things Pharaoh gave Joseph:

   a. Promotion (verses 40–41)

   b. Authority (verses 42–44)

   c. Name (verse 45a)

   d. Wife (verse 45b)

      (1) Notice that Pharaoh gave credit to God for Joseph's wisdom (verse 39). What does this suggest about Joseph's testimony before Pharaoh?

3. According to Genesis 41:46a, this event took place when Joseph was *thirty years old,* which means he was enslaved and in prison a total of thirteen years before he was released and promoted. Link this with the following Scriptures and note your insights:

   a. 1 Samuel 2:8a

b. Ecclesiastes 3:11a

c. 1 Peter 5:6

4. After his promotion, as a responsible prime minister, Joseph *went throughout all the land of Egypt* (Genesis 41:46b). Use Genesis 41:47–49, 53–57 to record your observations concerning Joseph's management of:

   a. The *seven plentiful years* (verses 47–49)

   b. The *seven years of famine* (verses 53–57)

5. It is interesting to note that Joseph gave Hebrew names to his *two sons* born before the *famine*, even though his wife was a high-ranking Egyptian (Genesis 41:50). Use Genesis 41:51–52 to consider the significance of their names:

	SIGNIFICANCE	YOUR THOUGHTS
Manasseh	Verse 51	
Ephraim	Verse 52	

a. Share a way God has helped you:

(1) *Forget* the past (see Philippians 3:13–14)

(2) Become *fruitful* in the midst of affliction (See Psalm 66:12b)

6. How does your study today speak to you concerning:

a. God's timing

b. God's sovereignty

c. God's purposes

SIXTH DAY: Review

1. Joseph went through some extenuating hardships before he was given such a powerful position in Pharaoh's court. Use the following circumstances to highlight Joseph's testings and how he triumphed:

   a. Slavery

   b. Responsibility over Potiphar's house

   c. Sexual temptation

   d. False accusation

   e. Imprisonment

2. What do you observe about Our Great Creator's activity throughout Joseph's testings?

NOTES

The Famine
GENESIS 42–43

FIRST DAY: Introduction

Romans 8:28 is one of the greatest assurances found in the Bible: *And we know that all things work together for good to those who love God, to those who are the called according to His purpose.*

Even when our circumstances seem dire, desperate, and disastrous, God is at work! Behind the scenes, God is weaving all the different elements of our lives together to fulfill His great and good plans for us.

In Genesis 42 and 43, the family of Jacob was in dire straights. They ran out of grain. The famine was devastating. Jacob had to send ten of his sons to Egypt to try to purchase grain. After a somewhat disastrous encounter with the prime minister of Egypt, Jacob's sons returned with grain, but without their brother Simeon. When the grain was finally consumed, the brothers were forced to return to Egypt. Jacob, at that moment, wrongly concluded, *All these things are against me* (Genesis 42:36). He had no idea how God was, and had been, working in all the tragedies of his life in order to save his whole family.

As the reader of this story, you have the advantage—you already know the miraculous movement of God in Joseph's life. Unfortunately, you do not have the same vantage point in your own circumstances. Nevertheless, the God of Jacob is still working in all the circumstances of your life for your ultimate good.

Take a moment to entrust any seemingly dire, desperate, or disastrous circumstances in your life to the Lord.

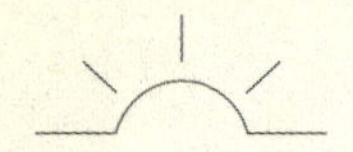

FOOD FOR THOUGHT

Famines were common in patriarchal times. Both Abraham (Genesis 12:10) and Isaac (Genesis 26:1) had to deal with famines.

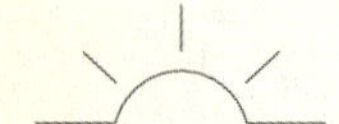

FOOD FOR THOUGHT

Egypt was about a three-week journey, 250–300 miles from Canaan.

SECOND DAY: Read Genesis 42:1–17

1. The great famine that was prophesied in Genesis 41 came to pass. Because it was so severe and widespread, it soon reached Jacob's family in Canaan. As a result, what did Jacob tell *his sons* to do? Genesis 42:1–2

2. *Joseph's ten brothers* did as their father asked (Genesis 42:3). However, why did Jacob *not send* Benjamin with them? Genesis 42:4

   a. What does Jacob's concern suggest?

3. The *sons of Israel went to buy grain* in Egypt, where they encountered Joseph. He was the one who sold grain *to all the people of the land* (Genesis 42:5–6a). Genesis 42:6b–17 captures the drama of their first interaction. Use these verses to note and comment on the following:

   a. The demeanor of Joseph's brothers (verses 6b, 8b)

   b. Joseph's demeanor (verses 7–8a)

   c. Joseph's recollection (verse 9a)

(1) Link this with Genesis 37:7, 9 and share your thoughts.

d. Joseph's accusations (verses 9b, 12, 14)

e. The claims of Joseph's brothers (verses 10–11, 13)

f. Joseph's test (verses 15–17)

(1) Why do you think Joseph put his brothers *in prison*?

(2) Considering how the brothers treated Joseph twenty years earlier, how would you describe Joseph's conduct toward them?

4. Share a way you see God's hand at work in the events portrayed in your study today.

THIRD DAY: Read Genesis 42:18–38

1. After keeping them in prison *three days*, Joseph spoke to his brothers. What do you find interesting about what Joseph acknowledged about himself? Genesis 42:18

   a. How would Joseph allow them to prove their innocence? Genesis 42:19–20a

2. Joseph's brothers had no choice to but comply (Genesis 42:20b). Why did they believe this was happening to them? Genesis 42:21

   a. What did Reuben say about the matter? Genesis 42:22

      (1) Even though it had been over twenty years since Joseph's brothers sold him into slavery, what does their reaction indicate?

         (a) What does this convey to you about the nature of unconfessed sin? See also Psalm 32:3–4.

3. Because Joseph *spoke to them through an interpreter*, they did not realize he understood them (Genesis 42:23). How did Joseph react to their words? Genesis 42:24a

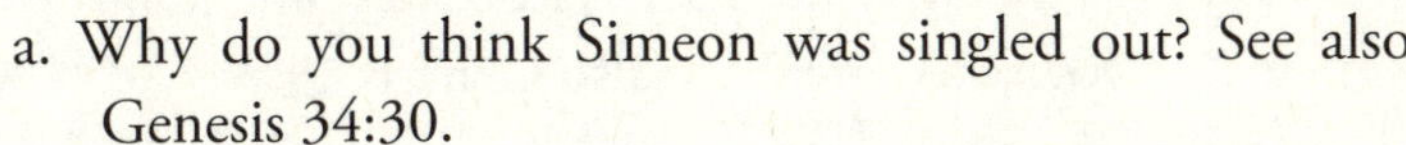

   a. Why do you think Simeon was singled out? See also Genesis 34:30.

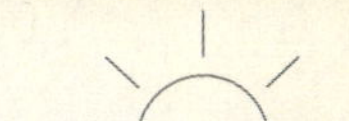

FOOD FOR THOUGHT

Joseph probably did not know about Reuben's attempt to save him until he overheard his brothers talking (Genesis 42:22–23).

4. From Genesis 42:25–38, share your insights about the following:

   a. Joseph's command (verse 25)

   b. The journey home (verses 26–28)

      (1) The brothers' reactions (verse 28b)

         (a) Why do you think they felt this way?

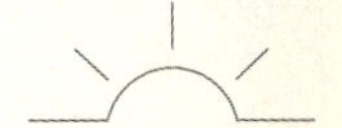

FOOD FOR THOUGHT

This is the first time in the narrative that Joseph's brothers mention God (Genesis 42:28).

   c. The brothers' report to Jacob (verses 29–35)

   d. Jacob's assessment (verses 36, 38)

e. Reuben's offer (verse 37)

(1) Why do you think Jacob was not appeased by Reuben's offer? See also Genesis 49:3–4.

5. Like Jacob, when in dire circumstances we are inclined to believe, *All these things are against me*. Yet, this is never true for a child of God. Use the following Scriptures to affirm what is true:

a. Psalm 56:9–11

b. Lamentations 3:31–33

c. Joel 2:25–26

d. Romans 8:31

FOURTH DAY: Read Genesis 43:1–14

1. According to Genesis 43:1–2, the *famine* continued to be *severe*, so when Jacob's family had *eaten up the grain* from Egypt, he told his sons to *go back* for more food. However, of what did Judah remind his father? Genesis 43:3–5

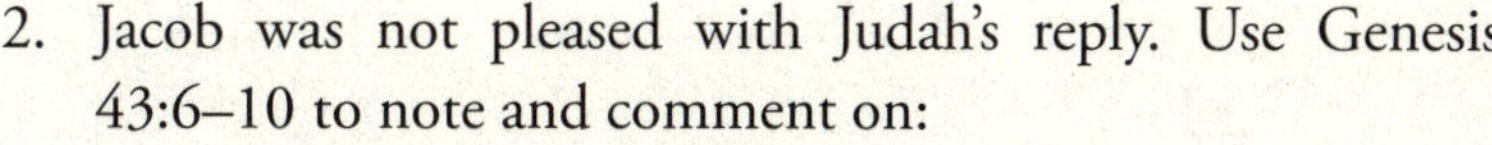

2. Jacob was not pleased with Judah's reply. Use Genesis 43:6–10 to note and comment on:

   a. Jacob's complaint (verse 6)

   b. His sons' explanation (verse 7)

   c. Judah's offer (verses 8–10)

      (1) What does this reveal about Judah?

3. Jacob finally acquiesced when he saw there was no other option. From Genesis 43:11–13 record the things he told his sons to *take* with them to Egypt:

   a. Verse 11

FOOD FOR THOUGHT

A famine is not a short-term situation. When sufficient rain finally falls, it still takes at least one full season before crops can produce enough grain.

b. Verse 12

c. Verse 13

(1) Why do you think Jacob did this?

4. Genesis 43:14 (NLT) says, *May God Almighty give you mercy as you go before the man, so that he will release Simeon and let Benjamin return. But if I must lose my children, so be it.* What do Jacob's words reveal about his perspective?

5. Jacob invoked the title *El Shaddai* (*God Almighty, the All-Sufficient One*). Why are these attributes of God crucial to remember when *all these things* seem to be against you?

FIFTH DAY: Read Genesis 43:15–34

1. Jacob's sons did as their father said, and brought the gifts, Benjamin, and *double money* with them *to Egypt*. Once more they *stood before Joseph* (Genesis 43:15). Use Genesis 43:16–23 to answer the following questions:

   a. What did Joseph do when he *saw Benjamin with them*? (verse 16)

b. When the *steward* brought the brothers to Joseph's house, why were they *afraid*? (verses 17–18)

c. What did they explain to the *steward*? (verses 19–22)

d. How did the *steward* respond? (verse 23)

(1) What does the steward's mention of God indicate to you?

2. According to Genesis 43:24, Joseph's brothers were given water to wash their *feet* and food for their *donkeys,* implying that they were honored guests in Joseph's home. What do you find remarkable about this?

3. Joseph's brothers then *made the present ready* for Joseph's arrival (Genesis 43:25). From Genesis 43:26–28, comment on their interaction *when Joseph came home.*

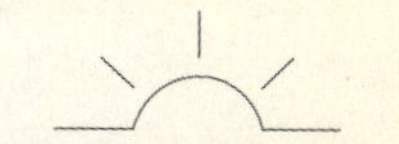

FOOD FOR THOUGHT

Ironically, Joseph's brothers were afraid they would be enslaved or imprisoned by Joseph—the very fate that they had constrained him to.

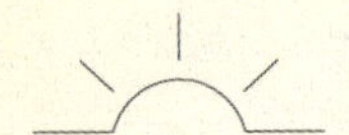

FOOD FOR THOUGHT

Benjamin is the only brother Joseph declared a blessing over (Genesis 43:29b).

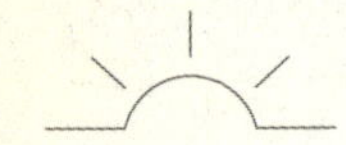

FOOD FOR THOUGHT

Dr. Henry Morris notes that the probability of randomly seating the eleven brothers according to their age was one in 39,941,000.[34]

4. Use Genesis 43:29–31 to describe Joseph's encounter with Benjamin.

5. Joseph's brothers then *ate with him*. Use Genesis 43:32–34 to note and remark on:

   a. Where they sat (verse 32)

   b. How they were seated (verse 33)

   c. How they were treated (verse 34)

      (1) Why do you think Joseph gave Benjamin more than his brothers?

      (2) Observe that Joseph's brothers *were merry with him* regardless of his favor toward Benjamin. Contrast this with the brothers' behavior in Genesis 37:3–4 and share why this is notable.

6. From your study today, what stands out most to you about Joseph's interaction with his brothers?

SIXTH DAY: Review

1. From your study this week, share a way you see God working in:

    a. The famine

    b. Joseph

    c. Judah

    d. Simeon

    e. Reuben

    f. The brothers

    g. Jacob

2. Using Genesis 42–43, share something you observed about the activity of Our Great Creator.

NOTES

Family Reunion

GENESIS 44–45

FIRST DAY: Introduction

God desires to reveal Himself to us, save us, provide for us, and bless us! However, He is unable to do this for us as long as our sin nature continues to dominate our thoughts and actions. God, in His grace, allows us to see the ugliness of our sin and repent. He often validates His redemptive work in us by testings to prove that our desires and heart have been changed. As we respond to His conviction, He begins to reveal Himself to us, that He might work His great goodness in and through our lives.

In a similar way, before Joseph revealed his identity to his brothers, he tested them. Joseph recognized that God had placed him in a powerful position in order *to preserve a posterity ... in the earth and to save ... by a great deliverance.* However, before Joseph could save his family, he had to verify that these men had truly changed. Genesis 44 records Joseph's final test and the repentant state of his brothers. What follows then in Genesis 45 is the great reveal.

Have you been tested by God? It is only because He wants to remove the dominating factor of sin from your life and bring His blessings in its stead.

Ask God to purify your heart that He might reveal Himself to you.

SECOND DAY: Read Genesis 44:1–14

1. As Joseph and his brothers enjoyed a meal at his home, Joseph arranged one final test using his brothers' relationship with Benjamin, the favored son. Use Genesis 44:1–14 to note and comment on:

   a. The set up (verses 1–2)

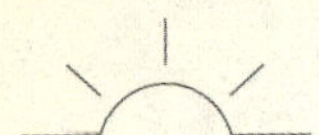

FOOD FOR THOUGHT

Genesis 40:8 and 41:16, 25 make it clear that Joseph credited God alone with divining powers. However, as part of a ruse to test his brothers, Joseph used a *cup of divination* as a prop.

b. The execution (verses 3–6)

c. The protest of innocence (verses 7–8)

d. The verdict (verses 9–10)

e. The search and discovery (verses 11–12)

f. The reaction (verses 13–14)

(1) Tearing *their clothes* signified deep distress. Why was their grief significant in this situation?

2. Contrast the demeanor of Joseph's brothers with their earlier conduct in Genesis 37:23–25a. What changes do you see in these men?

a. Why do you think it was necessary for Joseph to test his brothers?

THIRD DAY: Read Genesis 44:15–34

1. When Joseph's silver cup was found in Benjamin's possession, *Judah and his brothers* went back to Joseph's house and *fell before him* (Genesis 44:14). What did Joseph say to them? Genesis 44:15

   a. This was the third time Joseph's brothers bowed before him. Link this with Joseph's dream in Genesis 37:7 and share your thoughts.

2. According to Genesis 44:16 (NLT), Judah responded, *Oh, my lord, what can we say to you? How can we explain this? How can we prove our innocence? God is punishing us for our sins. My lord, we have all returned to be your slaves—all of us, not just our brother who had your cup in his sack.* What do you find remarkable about this response?

3. This was a critical moment for Joseph to assess whether his brothers cared more for Benjamin than for themselves. From Genesis 44:17 remark on how he tested them.

4. Judah responded with a heartfelt plea on behalf of Benjamin. Use Genesis 44:18–34 to note and comment on the following from Judah's speech:

   a. Judah's humility (verse 18)

b. Judah's explanation (verses 19–29)

c. Judah's concern (verses 30–31, 34)

d. Judah's promise (verse 32)

e. Judah's offer (verse 33)

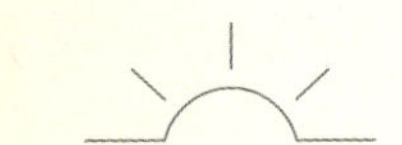

FOOD FOR THOUGHT

This is the longest recorded speech of any of Jacob's sons. It contains 218 Hebrew words. In this address, twelve times Judah referred to himself and his brothers as *your servants*.

(1) What does this speech suggest to you about Judah?

5. It is interesting that Jesus Christ came from the tribe of Judah. What Christlike qualities do you see in the example of Judah? See also John 15:13 and 1 John 3:16.

FOURTH DAY: Read Genesis 45:1–15

1. Upon hearing Judah's intercession for his brother Benjamin, Joseph *could not restrain himself* any longer and finally revealed his true identity. Use Genesis 45:1–4 to capture the drama of this great reveal:

a. The emotion (verses 1–2)

b. The revelation (verses 3a, 4)

c. The reaction (verse 3b)

(1) Recall that in many ways Joseph is a picture of Jesus. With this in mind, observe that Joseph's brothers were *dismayed in his presence*. Link this reaction with the prophecy concerning Jesus in Zechariah 12:10 and note any parallels you see.

2. Seeing his brothers' dismay, Joseph reassured them. From Genesis 45:5–8 note and remark on what Joseph explained to them about:

a. Their grief and anger at themselves (verse 5)

b. The *famine* (verses 6–7)

c. His position in Egypt (verse 8)

(1) Use Genesis 45:5, 7 to identify God's purposes in the things that had happened in Joseph's life:

(a) *for God sent me before you to* ___________ ______.

(b) *And God sent me before you to* ___________ __ ___________ *for you in the earth,*

(c) *and to* _________ _________ _________ *by a great deliverance.*

(2) What does this reveal about Joseph's perspective?

3. After reassuring his brothers, Joseph instructed them on what to do in light of the *famine*. Use Genesis 45:9–13 to answer the following questions:

   a. What did Joseph instruct concerning his *father*? (verses 9, 13)

   b. What was Joseph's plan to *provide* for them? (verses 10–11)

   c. What did Joseph reassure them of? (verse 12)

(1) Why do you think Joseph exhorted them to *hurry* with all these arrangements?

4. Remark on the picture of reconciliation recorded in Genesis 45:14–15.

   a. In verse 15 (NLT), Joseph's brothers *began talking freely with him*. Contrast this with Genesis 37:4b. What do you see?

5. Three times Joseph pointed out that God had *sent* him to Egypt for a purpose. Share a brief testimony of God's purpose in your life that was worked out through difficult circumstances.

6. Write a specific way that Joseph is an example to you.

FIFTH DAY: Read Genesis 45:16–28

1. The *report* of the arrival of Joseph's brothers reached *Pharaoh and his servants.* How did they react to this news? Genesis 45:16

   a. What did Pharaoh tell Joseph to do? Genesis 45:17–20

FOOD FOR THOUGHT

Pharaoh's instruction to Joseph showed the prominence, respect, and favor Joseph had in Egypt.

      (1) How do you see God working on behalf of Jacob's family?

2. The *sons of Israel* did as Pharaoh instructed (Genesis 45:21a). List the things Joseph *gave* them for their *journey.* Genesis 45:21b–23

   a. What do you note about Joseph's favoritism toward Benjamin?

3. As his brothers *departed* for Canaan, Joseph counseled them not to *become troubled along the way* (Genesis 45:24). Why do you think he said this?

4. Joseph's brothers left Egypt and *came to the land of Canaan to Jacob their father* (Genesis 45:25). What did they announce to Jacob? Genesis 45:26a

   a. For a moment, place yourself in Jacob's position. What had he been led to believe about Joseph? Genesis 37:33

      (1) How had he felt? Genesis 37:35

   b. Describe Jacob's initial reaction from Genesis 45:26b.

      (1) Why do you think he reacted this way?

   c. What convinced Jacob that his sons were telling the truth? Genesis 45:27

5. What does Jacob's statement convey about his attitude? Genesis 45:28

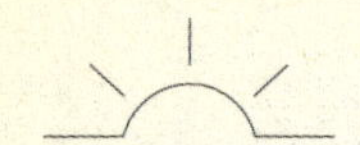

FOOD FOR THOUGHT

In Genesis 45:28 Jacob is called *Israel* for the first time since his name was changed by God (Genesis 35:10).

a. Recall that at one point Jacob declared, *All these things are against me* (Genesis 42:36b). What do you think he was beginning to realize?

(1) What divine truths about God do you need to realize in your life?

SIXTH DAY: Review

1. Our Great Creator is always working for our good. Use the following events from our lesson this week to note His activity in:

a. The brothers' testing

b. Joseph's hardships

c. The famine

d. Joseph's position in Egypt

2. How does this week's lesson inspire you concerning Our Great Creator's work in the events of your life?

NOTES

Journey to Egypt

GENESIS 46–48

FIRST DAY: Introduction

God desires to bless our lives! The paths to God's blessing are often circuitous and do not make sense to us at the time. However, God is always working to safeguard our inheritance, preserve and protect our lives, and bring His blessing.

Certainly, the path to blessing in Jacob's life was circuitous and seemingly senseless. Jacob had no idea of the ways in which God was working behind the scenes to safeguard his inheritance, preserve and protect his family, and bring them into all the blessings He had promised. In order to inherit God's blessing, Jacob had to lose his most beloved son for a time, leave the land of promise, and settle his whole clan in Egypt. Yet, God was in all these contrary circumstances, using all of them to fulfill the promises He made.

Do the circumstances in your life seem contrary to what God has promised? Submit them to God completely, that they may become the very pathways God will use to lead you into His blessings.

Submit any contrary circumstances of your life to God
that He might use them as a means to blessing.

SECOND DAY: Read Genesis 46

1. When Jacob (Israel) *took his journey with all that he had* on his way to meet Joseph, he stopped at the southernmost tip of the promised land, Beersheba. Beersheba had been a significant place in Abraham and Isaac's lives. It was also the place from which Jacob, some ninety years earlier, had fled from his brother Esau. When Jacob *came to Beersheba*, what did he do? Genesis 46:1b

   a. Connect this with Genesis 21:33 and 26:23–25. What do you see?

2. According to Genesis 46:2, the Lord *spoke to* Jacob *in the visions of the night*. Use Genesis 46:2b–4 to note and comment on:

   a. God's call (verse 2b)

   b. God's assurance (verse 3a)

   c. God's promises (verses 3b, 4b)

   d. God's presence (verse 4a)

(1) What significance do you think these promises held for Jacob?

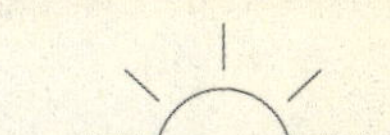

FOOD FOR THOUGHT

The phrase, *will put his hands on your eyes,* meant that Joseph would be present at Jacob's death.

3. From Genesis 46:5–7 briefly document the journey of Jacob's family to Egypt.

4. Genesis 46:8–27 recorded the family members who *went to Egypt*, noting that there were *seventy* (meaning Jacob's entire family at that time). As they approached Egypt, what did Jacob send Judah to do? Genesis 46:28

5. Jacob had not seen Joseph since he was seventeen. Joseph was now thirty-nine years old and an important official in Egypt. Use Genesis 46:29–30 to record this long-anticipated reunion.

   a. What blesses you most about this scene?

6. According to Genesis 46:31–32, what did Joseph say he would *tell Pharaoh*?

   a. Joseph advised his family to tell Pharaoh the same thing (Genesis 46:33–34a). Why would this enable them to *dwell in the land of Goshen*, apart from the Egyptians? Genesis 46:34b

      (1) Why do you think this was necessary? See also Deuteronomy 7:3–4a.

7. What portion of this chapter ministers to you the most?

THIRD DAY: Read Genesis 47:1–12

1. After his dramatic reunion with his family, *Joseph went and told Pharaoh* about them and their situation. He then *presented* five of his brothers to Pharaoh (Genesis 47:1–2). When Pharaoh asked their *occupation*, what was their response? Genesis 47:3–4

2. After hearing their request, what did Pharaoh offer Joseph? Genesis 47:5–6

   a. How do you see God's favor upon Joseph's family?

3. After this conversation between Pharaoh and Joseph's brothers, *Joseph brought in his father Jacob* (Genesis 47:7a). What did Jacob do? Genesis 47:7b

   a. Pharaoh was one of the greatest kings in the world at that time; in fact, in Egyptian religion, Pharaoh was considered a god. What does this convey to you about Jacob and his actions? See also Hebrews 7:7.

4. Remark on Jacob's commentary when Pharaoh asked him *how old* he was. Genesis 47:8–9

   a. Observe that Jacob referred to his life as a *pilgrimage*. Link this with Hebrews 11:9–10, 13–16 and share your thoughts.

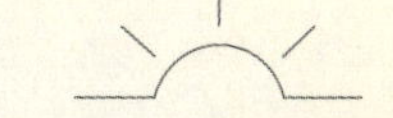

FOOD FOR THOUGHT

Goshen and the land of Rameses are synonymous after Joseph's reign. Pi Rameses (modern-day Qatar) was, for a time, the capital of the Egyptian Empire.

(1) How is this an example for believers? See Psalm 84:5 and 1 Peter 2:11.

5. From Genesis 47:11–12 record how Joseph:

   a. *Situated* his family (verse 11)

   b. *Provided* for his family (verse 12)

6. From your study today, share a way you see God's faithfulness to Jacob.

FOURTH DAY: Read Genesis 47:13–31

1. Although Joseph's family was taken care of, he still had to deal with the *famine*. From Genesis 47:13 describe the condition of the *land* at this time.

2. Genesis 47:14–21 documents how Joseph handled the *famine*. When the people came to him for help, comment on how Joseph managed:

   a. Their *money* (verses 14–15)

b. Their *livestock* (verses 16–17)

c. Their *bodies* and *lands* (verses 18–21)

(1) Identify the exception to this from Genesis 47:22.

3. According to Genesis 47:23, after Joseph *bought* the land of Egypt for Pharaoh, he gave the *people* seed to *sow the land.* What did he legislate for them? Genesis 47:24, 26

a. Remark on the people's response to these arrangements from Genesis 47:25. See also Proverbs 11:26.

(1) Share a way these events demonstrate Joseph's wisdom and leadership.

4. In contrast to the Egyptians, observe how Jacob and his family fared in Egypt (Genesis 47:27). What differences do you note?

5. Joseph spent the first *seventeen* years of his life with his father, Jacob. Use Genesis 47:28, to underscore God's faithfulness to Jacob during the last *seventeen* years of his life.

6. According to Genesis 47:29–31, what did Jacob make Joseph *swear*?

7. Commentator Henry Morris notes, *Jacob wanted even his burial to be a testimony to his faith in God's promises.*[35] How does Jacob's testimony of faith minister to you? See also Hebrews 11:13.

FIFTH DAY: Read Genesis 48

1. *Now it came to pass,* after Joseph heard that Jacob was *sick*, he took *his two sons* to see him. When Jacob heard they were coming, he *strengthened himself and sat up on the bed* to speak to them (Genesis 48:1–2). Use Genesis 48:3–7 to note and comment on what Jacob said concerning:

   a. God Almighty (verses 3–4)

   b. Ephraim and Manasseh (verse 5)

   c. Joseph's future *offspring* (verse 6)

d. Rachel (verse 7)

2. Jacob then turned his attention to *Joseph's sons* (Genesis 48:8). Use Genesis 48:9–10 to describe how Joseph presented his sons to Jacob.

a. From Genesis 48:11, record Jacob's exclamation.

(1) Connect this with Ephesians 3:20 and share your thoughts.

3. Joseph brought his sons forward, placing the eldest, Manasseh, at his father's *right hand*, and Ephraim at his *left hand* (Genesis 48:12–13). According to Hebrews 11:21, what did Jacob *knowingly* do by faith? Genesis 48:14

4. Beginning with a beautiful description of God, Jacob *blessed Joseph*. Use Genesis 48:15–16a to fill in the blanks with this description:

a. ______, *before whom my fathers* ______________ *and* ________________ *walked.*

b. *The God who has fed me all my* __________ ________

to this ________.

(1) The word Jacob used for *fed* is the Hebrew word *ra'ah*, which means *to shepherd*; it is the first time in Scripture God is referred to as our shepherd. Link this with Psalm 23:1 and John 10:11, 14 and share what this description of God means to you.

c. *The* ________ *who has* ______________

me from ________ _________.

(1) This is the first usage in Scripture of the Hebrew word *ga'al* (*to redeem*). Why do you think it is significant that this is used in reference to Jacob's circumstances?

5. Use Genesis 48:16b to cite and remark on the rest of Jacob's blessing upon *the lads*.

6. How did Joseph react when his *father laid his right hand* on the younger son, Ephraim? Genesis 48:17–18

a. What did Jacob prophesy in response? Genesis 48:19

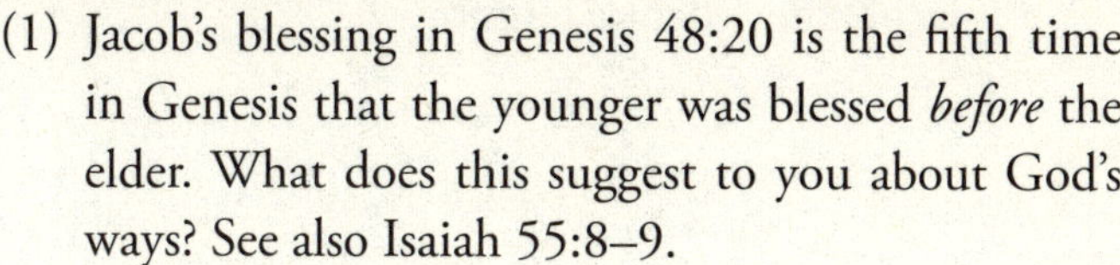

(1) Jacob's blessing in Genesis 48:20 is the fifth time in Genesis that the younger was blessed *before* the elder. What does this suggest to you about God's ways? See also Isaiah 55:8–9.

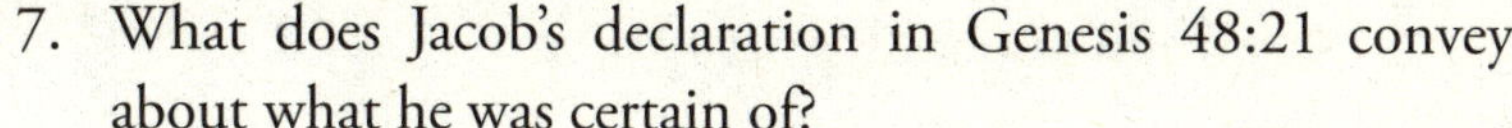

7. What does Jacob's declaration in Genesis 48:21 convey about what he was certain of?

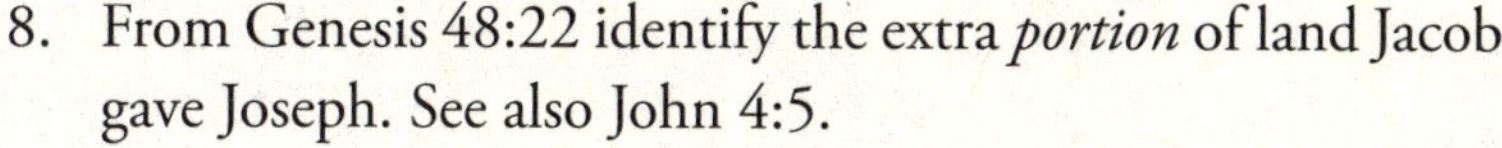

8. From Genesis 48:22 identify the extra *portion* of land Jacob gave Joseph. See also John 4:5.

9. Share a brief testimony of how God has:

   a. Fed (shepherded) you all your life long

   b. Redeemed you from all evil

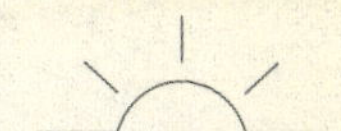

FOOD FOR THOUGHT

Not only did Ephraim become a greater tribe than Manasseh, but several times in the Old Testament the entire Northern Kingdom of Israel is referred to as Ephraim. Joshua, who would lead the children of Israel back into the Promised Land, was from the tribe of Ephraim.

SIXTH DAY: Review

1. From your study this week, share something that stood out to you concerning:

   a. Jacob and Joseph's reunion

   b. Joseph's leadership

   c. Jacob and his family's occupation

   d. Jacob's faith

   e. Jacob's blessing

2. How are you encouraged by the seemingly circuitous ways of Our Great Creator?

NOTES

NOTES

The Blessing

GENESIS 49–50

FIRST DAY: Introduction

There is nothing as wonderful as God's blessing on our lives! The book of Genesis begins and ends with God's blessing. In the beginning, God blessed His new creation. However, with the intrusion of sin, mankind and the earth fell under a curse. The last chapter of Genesis reminds us that God is able to overcome what is meant for evil (the curse) and use it for good (a blessing). This is clearly seen in the crucifixion; Jesus took the curse of sin that we might receive the blessing of God. Now we have been blessed *with every spiritual blessing in the heavenly places* (Ephesians 1:3).

As a young man, Jacob was desperate for his father's blessing. In order to receive that blessing, Jacob resorted to deceit and trickery. At the end of his life, Jacob, knowing the value of a blessing, blessed his sons before he died. In turn, Joseph, rather than retaliate for the harm his brothers had done to him, chose to bless and be a blessing to his brothers.

First Peter 3:9 reminds us that *not returning evil for evil or reviling for reviling, but on the contrary blessing, knowing that you were called to this, that you may inherit a blessing.* Our God is a blessing God and has called us to be blessed, be a blessing, and bless others.

Ask God to make you a blessing
and use you to bring His blessing to others.

SECOND DAY: Read Genesis 49:1–12

1. As Jacob was dying, he called his sons and said, *Gather together that I may tell you what shall befall you in the last days* (Genesis 49:1–2). Jacob's prophetic words were a synopsis of his sons' weaknesses and strengths. These men would each become a tribe in Israel with a specific allotment in the Promised Land and specific tribal tendencies. Jacob began his blessing with the first four sons of Leah. Use Genesis 49:3–12 to note and comment on the weaknesses and strengths of:

   a. Reuben (verses 3–4)

      (1) According to 1 Chronicles 5:1, Reuben's sin cost him the birthright of the firstborn. What's more, true to Jacob's prophecy, the tribe of Reuben never produced any leaders nor excelled in any way. What warning or lesson do you receive from the life and character of Reuben?

   b. Simeon and Levi (verses 5–7)

      (1) Review Genesis 34:25–30 and remark on Jacob's rebuke.

(2) True to what Jacob prophesied, when Israel settled in the land of Canaan, Judah essentially absorbed Simeon's inheritance, and Levi was scattered among the other tribes. However, God appointed the Levites to be the priestly tribe that represented Him and ministered to the spiritual needs of the people throughout the land. What does this convey to you about God's mercy?

FOOD FOR THOUGHT

Note that even though Jacob cursed Simeon and Levi's anger (Genesis 49:7), he did not remove these two sons from the covenant blessing.

c. Judah (verses 8–12)

(1) Jacob's word to Judah was a powerful Messianic prophecy concerning Jesus Christ. Use these verses to fill in the chart:

PROPHECY	CROSS REFERENCE	YOUR INSIGHTS
Verse 8	1 Chronicles 5:2, Philippians 2:10–11	
Verse 9	Revelation 5:5	
Verse 10	Jeremiah 23:5–6, Luke 1:31–33, Hebrews 1:8	
Verses 11–12	Isaiah 63:1–3, Matthew 21:5–9	

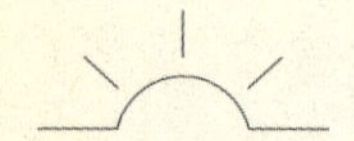

FOOD FOR THOUGHT

Isaiah 9:6–7 declares that Jesus is our *Prince of Peace and of His government and peace there will be no end.*

(2) The name *Shiloh* refers to peace, but can also be translated *He whose right it is*. How do you see both of these descriptions applying to Jesus?

2. From your study today, what stands out to you from Jacob's prophecies?

THIRD DAY: Read Genesis 49:13–28

1. After pronouncing a blessing upon the first four sons of Leah, Jacob proceeded to bless the rest of his sons. Choose phrases from Genesis 49:13–27 that describe:

   a. Zebulun (verse 13)

   b. Issachar (verses 14–15)

   c. Dan (verses 16–18)

      (1) Jacob's exclamation in verse 18 contains the first usage in the Bible of the Hebrew word *Yeshua*, which means *salvation*. The names *Joshua* and *Jesus* are derived from this word. What do you find significant about this?

d. Gad (verse 19)

e. Asher (verse 20)

f. Naphtali (verse 21)

g. Joseph (verses 22–26)

(1) Because of Reuben's sin, Jacob blessed Joseph with the birthright (1 Chronicles 5:1). Comment on the extent of this blessing.

(2) In his blessing upon Joseph, Jacob proclaimed five attributes of God. Use verses 24–25 to list and remark on these names:

(a) Verse 24

1.

2.

3.

(b) Verse 25

4.

5.

(c) Which of these attributes ministers to you presently?

h. Benjamin (verse 27)

2. Jacob conferred the blessing God gave Abraham to all of his sons. The Hebrew word for *bless* is *barak,* and is the act of bringing God's favor upon someone's life. What does Genesis 49:28 say about the way in which Jacob blessed his sons?

a. Link Jacob's blessing with Galatians 3:14. What do you see?

FOURTH DAY: Read Genesis 49:29–50:14

1. After blessing his sons, Jacob gave them a final charge concerning his burial. Use Genesis 49:29–32 to describe where Jacob wanted to be *buried.*

a. *The cave that is in the field of Machpelah* was the only piece of land Abraham owned in Canaan. Bible scholar Henry Morris said of this, *It was to be a testimony to the generations to come, that Abraham, Isaac, and Jacob had faith in God's promise that He would give the land to their seed.*[36] How does this highlight why Jacob wanted to be buried there?

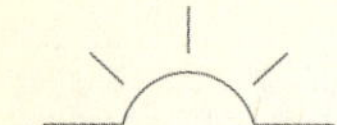

FOOD FOR THOUGHT

The traits that Jacob prophesied in blessing his sons were reiterated 400 years later by Moses in Deuteronomy 33 when he blessed the tribes of Israel.

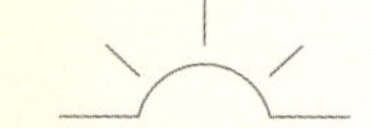

FOOD FOR THOUGHT

Five of Jacob's twelve sons were compared to animals:
Judah—lion
Issachar—donkey
Dan—serpent
Naphtali—deer
Benjamin—wolf

2. From Genesis 49:33, record the death of Jacob.

   a. How did Joseph react to his father's death? Genesis 50:1

   b. How is this a fulfillment of God's promise to Jacob in Genesis 46:4?

3. Genesis 50:2–14 records the burial of Jacob. Use these verses to remark on:

   a. The embalming (verses 2–3)

   b. The permission (verses 4–6)

   c. The procession (verses 7–9)

   d. The mourning (verses 10–11)

   e. The burial (verses 12–14)

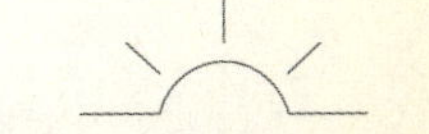

FOOD FOR THOUGHT

The Egyptians mourned for Jacob seventy days. The mourning period for a Pharaoh in Egypt was seventy-two days.

4. Take a moment to review Jacob's testimony from the following Scriptures:

   a. Genesis 28:16–22

   b. Genesis 31:38–42

   c. Genesis 32:9–10, 24–30

   d. Genesis 35:2–3

   e. Genesis 48:15–16a

      (1) To sum up this testimony, write an epitaph for Jacob.

FIFTH DAY: Read Genesis 50:15–26

1. After they had buried their father Jacob, *Joseph's brothers* became concerned about their standing with Joseph. Use Genesis 50:15–21 to observe and comment on:

   a. Their fear (verse 15)

   b. Their plea (verses 16–18)

      (1) By what means did they convey their plea to Joseph?

   c. Joseph's response (verses 17b, 19–21)

      (1) Why do you think Joseph *wept* at his brothers' words?

      (2) Use Luke 23:34 and Acts 4:10–12 to underscore Joseph's Christlike example.

(3) How do you see God overcoming man's *evil* intent with His good purposes?

(a) How does the reality of God's overcoming power minister to you?

2. Genesis 50:22–23 records that Joseph had an influence in the lives of his grandchildren and great grandchildren. Considering his life and legacy, what type of influence do you suppose he had on them?

3. Link Joseph's request in Genesis 50:24–25 with Hebrews 11:22. What do you see?

4. According to Genesis 50:26, Joseph died at the age of 110 and was *embalmed* and placed *in a coffin in Egypt*. As discussed previously, Joseph's life is in many ways a picture of Jesus. As you consider the life of Joseph, which aspect of his Christlike example:

   a. Ministers to you

b. Challenges you

SIXTH DAY: Review

1. God desires to bless! Using your lesson this week, answer the following questions:

    a. How did Jacob bless his sons?

    b. What kept some of his sons from greater blessing?

    c. In what ways was Joseph a blessing to his brothers?

    d. What did you observe concerning God's blessing overcoming man's evil?

2. What does it mean to you that Our Great Creator is a blessing God?

NOTES

NOTES

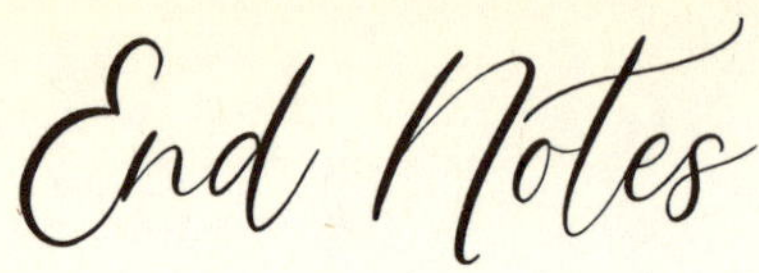

1. Guzik, David. "Study Guide for Genesis 1." Blue Letter Bible. 21 Feb, 2017. Web. 11 Jul, 2019. <https://www.blueletterbible.org/Comm/guzik_david/StudyGuide2017-Gen/Gen-1.cfm>.

2. Guzik, David. "Study Guide for Genesis 2." Blue Letter Bible. 21 Feb, 2017. Web. 11 Jul, 2019. <https://www.blueletterbible.org/Comm/guzik_david/StudyGuide2017-Gen/Gen-2.cfm>.

3. Guzik, David. "Study Guide for Genesis 3." Blue Letter Bible. 21 Feb, 2017. Web. 11 Jul, 2019. <https://www.blueletterbible.org/Comm/guzik_david/StudyGuide2017-Gen/Gen-3.cfm>.

4. McGee, J. Vernon. *Genesis: Volume 1.* Pasadena, CA: Thru the Bible Books, 1984. Print, p. 100.

5. Ibid., p. 98.

6. Smith, Chuck. "C2000 Series on Genesis 2-3." Blue Letter Bible. 1 Jun, 2005. Web. 11 Jul, 2019. <https://www.blueletterbible.org/Comm/smith_chuck/c2000_Gen/Gen_002.cfm>.

7. Wiersbe, Warren. *The Transformation Study Bible.* Colorado Springs, CO: David C. Cook, 2009. Print, p. 12.

8. Ibid., p. 106

9. Guzik, David. "Study Guide for Genesis 6." Blue Letter Bible. 21 Feb, 2017. Web. 11 Jul, 2019. <https://www.blueletterbible.org/Comm/guzik_david/StudyGuide2017-Gen/Gen-6.cfm>.

10. *The Life Application Study Bible.* Carol Stream, IL: Tyndale House Publishers, 2015. Print, p. 23.

11. Guzik, David. "Study Guide for Genesis 9." Blue Letter Bible. 21 Feb, 2017. Web. 11 Jul, 2019. <https://www.blueletterbible.org/Comm/guzik_david/StudyGuide2017-Gen/Gen-9.cfm>.

12. Morris, Henry. *The Genesis Record.* Grand Rapids, MI: Baker Books, 1976. Print, p. 273.

13. Wiersbe, Warren. *The Transformation Study Bible.* Colorado Springs, CO: David C. Cook, 2009. Print, p. 24.

14. Ibid., p. 28.

15. *The HCSB Study Bible.* Nashville, TN: Holman Bible Publishers, 2010. Print, p. 30.

16. Chambers, Oswald. *Not Knowing Where.* Grand Rapids, MI: Discovery House Publishers, 1989. Print, p. 61.

17. *The NLT Study Bible.* Carol Stream, IL: Tyndale House Publishers, 2017. Print, p. 56.

18. Guzik, David. "Study Guide for Genesis 18." Blue Letter Bible. 21 Feb, 2017. Web. 11 Jul, 2019. <https://www.blueletterbible.org/Comm/guzik_david/StudyGuide2017-Gen/Gen-18.cfm>.

19. Smith, Chuck. "C2000 Series on Genesis 19–20." Blue Letter Bible. 1 Jun, 2005. Web. 11 Jul, 2019. <https://www.blueletterbible.org/Comm/smith_chuck/c2000_Gen/Gen_019.cfm>.

20. Wiersbe, Warren. *The Transformation Study Bible.* Colorado Springs, CO: David C. Cook, 2009. Print, p. 38.

21. Smith, Chuck. "C2000 Series on Genesis 19–20." Blue Letter Bible. 1 Jun, 2005. Web. 11 Jul, 2019. <https://www.blueletterbible.org/Comm/smith_chuck/c2000_Gen/Gen_019.cfm>.

22. McGee, J. Vernon. *Genesis: Volume 2.* Pasadena, CA: Thru the Bible Books, 1984. Print, p. 35.

23. Wiersbe, Warren. *The Transformation Study Bible.* Colorado Springs, CO: David C. Cook, 2009. Print, p. 44.

24. Guzik, David. "Study Guide for Genesis 22." Blue Letter Bible. 21 Feb, 2017. Web. 11 Jul, 2019. <https://www.blueletterbible.org/Comm/guzik_david/StudyGuide2017-Gen/Gen-22.cfm>.

25. McGee, J. Vernon. *Genesis: Volume 2.* Pasadena, CA: Thru the Bible Books, 1984. Print, p. 64.

26. Guzik, David. "Study Guide for Genesis 22." Blue Letter Bible. 21 Feb, 2017. Web. 11 Jul, 2019. <https://www.blueletterbible.org/Comm/guzik_david/StudyGuide2017-Gen/Gen-22.cfm>.

27. Smith, Chuck. "C2000 Series on Genesis 24–26." Blue Letter Bible. 1 Jun, 2005. Web. 11 Jul, 2019. <https://www.blueletterbible.org/Comm/smith_chuck/c2000_Gen/Gen_024.cfm>.

28. Wiersbe, Warren. *The Transformation Study Bible.* Colorado Springs, CO: David C. Cook, 2009. Print, p. 49.

29. Ibid., p. 55.

30. Henry, Matthew. "Commentary on Genesis 28." Blue Letter Bible. 1 Mar, 1996. Web. 11 Jul, 2019. <https://www.blueletterbible.org/Comm/mhc/Gen/Gen_028.cfm>.

31. Wiersbe, Warren. *The Transformation Study Bible.* Colorado Springs, CO: David C. Cook, 2009. Print, p. 65.

32. Smith, Chuck. "C2000 Series on Genesis 32–36." Blue Letter Bible. 1 Jun, 2005. Web. 11 Jul, 2019. <https://www.blueletterbible.org/Comm/smith_chuck/c2000_Gen/Gen_032.cfm>.

33. Guzik, David. "Study Guide for Genesis 34." Blue Letter Bible. 21 Feb, 2017. Web. 11 Jul, 2019. <https://www.blueletterbible.org/Comm/guzik_david/StudyGuide2017-Gen/Gen-34.cfm>.

34. Morris, Henry. *The Genesis Record.* Grand Rapids, MI: Baker Books, 1976. Print, p. 610.

35. Ibid., p. 643.

36. Ibid., p. 662.

For it is the *God* who commanded light
to shine out of darkness,
who has shone in our hearts
to give the light of the knowledge of the glory of God
in the face of *Jesus Christ*.

—2 Corinthians 4:6